Dancing on the Tightrope

"We can all lead more joy-filled and meaningful lives. True joy is lurking around the corner. You can discover it, feel it and spread it. Kudos to Beth Kurland for penning an illuminating book. Read it, follow the sage advice. It will open and expand your heart and help you embrace this precious life to its fullest." —**Sanjiv Chopra,** Best Selling Author
Professor of Medicine, Harvard Medical School

"Dr. Kurland provides a penetrating analysis of our Stone Age brain and its challenges in the twenty-first century. Then with great clarity and heart, she explains how to deal with these and be more mindful, resilient, and happy right in the middle of everyday life. Her voice is warm and friendly, like chatting with a good friend who happens to be a wonderful therapist. A useful, beautiful book." —**Rick Hanson, Ph.D.**, author of
Resilient: How to Grow an Unshakable Core of
Calm, Strength, and Happiness

"This book will help you develop your inner resources, and the confidence that you can find balance and joy amidst all seasons of life. Highly recommended!" —**Tara Brach**, author of
Radical Acceptance and True Refuge

"An honest, accessible and compassionate manual for relaxing the grip of our brain-based reactivity in daily life. With a gentle touch and practical clarity, Beth Kurland illuminates the self-protective habits that make us unhappy, and guides readers in cultivating kinder practices as antidotes to these reactive patterns our brains bring our way—Dr. Kurland's practices and insight support the gradual, skillful process of opening our hearts to the truth of our experience." —**Mitch Abblett, Ph.D.**, author of
The Five Hurdles to Happiness...and the
Mindful Path for Overcoming Them

"POWERFUL AND TIMELY! This is a must read for anyone interested in mindfulness, personal development, or conscious evolution! In her book, Beth Kurland brings mindfulness to a new level. Didn't think there was another level? Guess again. Kurland discusses the neuroscience behind what she calls our evolutionary challenges. Full of real life scenarios to illustrate the ways in which mindfulness can help us overcome these evolutionary challenges, Kurland points the reader toward a more evolved way of being in the world. An informative, easy read that could just as easily find its way onto a required reading list at college level classes as it could onto the bedside table of personal growth enthusiasts."

—**Kathleen Mackenzie**, Ed.D., LICSW
Senior Lecturer Behavioral Science Program
Northeastern University

"In her latest book, Beth Kurland offers a wonderful resource that normalizes the inevitable adversity and life challenges we all face, elucidates the habits of our minds that detract from our ability to live our best lives, and outlines steps we can take to address them productively and in ways that lead to inner peace. Her years of experience as a clinical psychologist fortify every page. The personal stories from her own life make the text relatable, and embedded throughout are opportunities to write and reflect, allowing the reader to chart a plan that puts them on a path toward greater well-being. Resilience and psychological strength are skills that can be learned, and Beth Kurland's book is an excellent place to start."

—**Tim Bono**, Ph.D.
Assistant Dean and Lecturer in Psychology at
Washington University in St. Louis
Author of *When Likes Aren't Enough:*
A Crash Course in the Science of Happiness

"*Dancing on the Tightrope* is ultimately a book about hope. Kurland masterfully weaves together practical exercises, personal narrative, brain science, and concrete examples from her work as a therapist to show us that we have the power to change the way we show up in the world. She explains five evolutionary challenges that keep us trapped in unhelpful, reactive patterns of thought and behavior, and then provides the antidote—five practical tools that illuminate and illustrate the path into a "wide-awake" life of intentional, healthy, non-reactive living, full of connection to others and ultimately to ourselves. This is a must-read for those seeking to begin or deepen a practice of mindful, conscious living."

—**David Ronka**
Presenter, Kripalu Center for Yoga and Health
Author of *The Flipside of Fear*

"Dancing on the Tightrope shines a bright light on making life simpler and more enjoyable through the practice of mindfulness. Dr. Kurland presents a practical and unique plan for developing our resilience and awareness while guiding ourselves through everyday challenges."

—**Mark Bertin, M.D.**, Developmental Pediatrics
Author, *Mindful Parenting for*
ADHD and How Children Thrive
www.developmentaldoctor.com

dancing on the tightrope

OTHER BOOKS BY BETH KURLAND, PhD

The Transformative Power of Ten Minutes:
An Eight Week Guide to Reducing Stress
and Cultivating Well-Being

∽

Gifts of the Rain Puddle:
Poems, Meditations and Reflections for
the Mindful Soul

dancing on the tightrope

transcending the habits of your mind & awakening to your fullest life

BETH KURLAND, PhD

WELLBRIDGE BOOKS
An Imprint of Six Degrees Publishing Group
Portland · Oregon

Published in the USA by WELLBRIDGE BOOKS
an Imprint of Six Degrees Publishing Group

ISBN: 978-1-942497-43-1
Ebook ISBN: 978-1-942497-44-8
LCCN: 2018957966

Cover Design and Art: Kathleen Lynch, BLACK KAT DESIGN
Interior Layout: Denise C. Williams

Disclaimer: This publication is designed as a source of information only and is not intended as a substitute for psychological treatment or professional services of any kind. The author and the publisher expressly disclaim responsibility for any adverse effects arising from the use or application of the information contained herein. If mental health treatment is required, readers should seek individual help and services from a licensed mental health professional.

Author's Note: The people in this book were drawn from a composite of patients I have known over the years, as well as from some of my own personal experiences. Resemblance to any one person is purely coincidental. All identities have been disguised, and real names and identifying information is not used.

To Dad—
for your resilience that is an inspiration to us all,
and for encouraging me to be my best self.

To Alan, Rachel and Noah —
You are my happiest place on this shared journey of life.
You are all nothing less than amazing.

CONTENTS

ACKNOWLEDGMENTS

THE IDEA FOR WRITING THIS BOOK grew out of the workshops and public speaking that I have done in recent years, as I have sought to find ways of teaching larger audiences the tools I am most passionate about. It also grew out of my deepest wish to help others discover how to navigate life's challenges with greater ease and find wholeness and joy in their day-to-day lives. It is, in part, an accumulation and synthesis of what I have learned from many great teachers over the years from within and outside of the field of psychology, and from my many mentors and therapists and colleagues along my journey. One of the many benefits of working on this book is that it has been a daily reminder for me to use the tools that I teach, to help me with my own reactive patterns and habits of my mind that I get stuck in. I want to acknowledge this common humanity that we all share, and I hope that reading this book will help others not feel so alone in their struggles.

Over the years I have been deeply influenced by the work of so many others in my field, and I would like to acknowledge a few people who have been particularly influential to me. I had the privilege of taking several extensive online courses with Rick Hanson, and his teachings and writings have been inspirational throughout this book and in my work with my patients. My mentor from my internship, Robert Brooks, first introduced me to the idea of helping others grow resilience about 25 years ago, and his teaching and writing has continued to resonate deeply with me through the years. I would like to extend a special thanks to Tara Brach for sharing her wisdom with the world. Her talks, meditations and books have been both a deep source of learning for me, as well as a source of comfort and solace. I would like to gratefully acknowledge the work of Daniel Siegel, Kelly McGonigal, Barbara Fredrickson, Kristen Neff, Sharon Salzberg, Ronald Siegel, Richard Davidson, Jon Kabat-Zinn, and Herbert Benson, for their wonderful contributions to the field of psychology. There are so many others who go unnamed here, but to whom I am grateful for all that I have learned from them.

Please know that I have done my best to accurately explain all of the scientific and psychological concepts that I talk about in this book, but with the field always growing and expanding, I am sure that there may be new information I missed, or new information that will be coming out after this book is published. I found myself discovering so many new books even just in the past month and wishing I could tweak and edit my manuscript indefinitely to incorporate all of this information.

My very deepest appreciation goes out to all of the people who took time out of their very rich and busy lives to review this book: Rick Hanson, Sanjiv Chopra, Tara Brach, Mitch Abblett, Kathleen McKenzie, Tim Bono, David Ronka, and Mark Bertin. I can't express how much it meant to me for each of these amazing people to be willing to read my manuscript. Thank you for your generosity!

This book would not be possible without a lot of behind the scenes help. I want to send out a huge thank you to my editor, Allison Jones, who has a true gift with words and spent countless hours with this manuscript. I am so grateful for her expertise and help!

I would like to express my deepest gratitude to my publisher Denise Williams of WellBridge Books, who truly made this book possible. This is my third book with Denise and it is an absolute pleasure and privilege to have this opportunity to work with her again! I thank her for her patience with all of my "this one is the final draft" emails, and for her extraordinary skill and expertise in pulling all of this together and making it seem so effortless (when I know it is anything but that). I am truly grateful for all that she does.

A huge thank you goes out to Kathleen Lynch, for designing my book cover. I am honored and blessed to have Kathleen's artistic talents as the face of my book! While it may be true that you can't always judge a book by its cover, in this case I hope that people do judge my book by its amazing cover. Thank you Kathleen!

I feel so fortunate to have the support of such wonderful colleagues and friends! Thank you to all of my colleagues at Child and Family Psychological Services. I am grateful to be affiliated with such skilled clinicians. Thank you to Kristen Lee for her support, help, and inspiration with her awesome books. Thank you to Paul Block for an ongoing collegial relationship and friendship that I greatly value. A special thank you to my dear friend and colleague Shari Engelbourg, whom I have known for 23 years, and with whom I have the privilege of sharing this work and leading workshops together. Thank you to my wonderful therapists over the years that have helped me in invaluable ways, and to all of those people in my life who support my emotional and physical well-being.

A gigantic thank you to ALL of my friends who have enriched my life, shared in my joys and sorrows, and offered support, friendship and companionship over the years. I am truly blessed to have so many wonderful people in my life and I send out a huge hug to each and every one of you!

A special thanks is in order to all of my friends and family members who were dragged into my title dilemma for a good month or two. The persons who bore the brunt of this were my sister, Cindy, and my husband Alan (who had endless patience to go over titles well into the night), but my entire family, all of my friends who patiently listened to title after title (you know who you are), and even my son's friends who helped vote on some titles — thank you for your input, and for putting up with me.

A few very big acknowledgments are in order for my family members. Words cannot express my gratitude to my husband Alan, whom I have been blessed to have as my life partner for more than half of my life now. Alan is one of those extraordinary people who always has the time for me, no matter how stressful and crazily busy his life might be, and who is able to be fully present and give his undivided attention whenever you need. (He is like this not just with family and friends, but with his patients as well). His infinite emotional support, patience even when I have lost mine, sense of humor, and ongoing encouragement with everything I do, is a constant source of strength for me.

My stepmom, Eve Siegel, has been there for me every step of the way, from reading my first draft and encouraging me to pursue writing this book, to fielding phone calls of all kinds on an ongoing basis, offering advice and support that has been invaluable. My sister Cindy deserves a gold medal for her patience and generosity of her time in helping me with every aspect of this book and in being best friend, skilled psychologist and consultant, and at times my personal "therapist." She gives new meaning to the phrase "the wind beneath my wings."

My father, Lewis Siegel, has been one of my greatest role models, and someone I have only grown to admire more and more over the years. My dad is a man of true integrity and the values he taught me and lives by have become a cornerstone in my life. I am so thankful for all of my dad's love and support throughout my life. My brother Mike Siegel, has been my life long friend and one of the people I most admire in his ability to take scientific knowledge and bring about widespread, positive change. I am so grateful for my in-laws, Susan and Ray Kurland, who offer me ongoing love and support and share such excitement for all of my professional endeavors. How fortunate am I to have an amazing family of sister and brother in-laws, and nieces and nephews, who are all extraordinary people, and who enrich my life in so many ways. A special expression of gratitude to my children, Rachel and Noah, who are two of my greatest teachers, and make the world a better place by their loving presence. And a whisper of thanks to my mother, who is no longer here, but is always with me in my heart.

These acknowledgments would not be complete without expressing my gratitude to *all* of my patients over the years, whose strength and resilience have taught me and inspired me. I feel so fortunate to call what I do "work" when it is so fulfilling and rewarding.

And to you, my readers — thank you for your interest in picking up this book. I hope you will find that this book contributes to your life in a meaningful and significant way. I wish for you much well-being!

PREFACE

O VER THE PAST FEW YEARS, I have had a recurring dream. In the dream, I am in my house, but I suddenly discover that there are all of these unused rooms that I completely forgot existed. As I walk through these re-discovered rooms I realize how much open space I have, that I never knew was there, but in fact was there all along. I feel a sense of curiosity, joy, and excitement.

Our lives are like this, I believe. I know my life has been like this. Similar to many people, I lived in a small, familiar space made up of my habits and automatic programs, my old conditioning, and my limited beliefs about who I thought I was and what I was lacking. My stress, anxiety and worries often overshadowed the joy and peace that was possible. Sometimes it still does. But over the years I have learned ways to loosen the grip of old patterns that no longer serve me and I have discovered the freedom that comes as a result. This journey has been both a very personal one, and a professional one as I have put into practice, for myself and my patients, teachings from psychology and neuroscience, as well as mind-body approaches to healing and well-being. Not only have I experienced a gradual transformation in my own life, but I also have had the privilege of witnessing the transformation of so many of my patients. I am excited to share with you what I have learned.

Often we remain confined in the small spaces of our house, unaware of the other rooms that exist. Our negative thinking, self-doubt, feelings of unworthiness, automatic-pilot mode of going through the motions of our day, and some of the more primitive operating systems of our brain, contribute to this limited experience of life. To encounter the wholeness of our lives and the joy and fullness that is possible, we don't have to go looking for another house. We just need to know how to find our way to the hidden rooms to rediscover what was there all along. This book will show you how.

My intention in writing this book is to give you a window into what is possible in your life, and the tools to fully inhabit the wholeness of who you are and enjoy all life has to offer. I invite you to discover for yourself what might be available when you recognize what is holding you back and learn to work through those obstacles. I hope you'll come along for the journey!

—Beth Kurland, Ph.D.

INTRODUCTION

Dancing on the Tightrope

I AM SITTING in a small, outdoor café with my father and stepmom. We had recently finished yet another conversation about possible titles for this book. The topic had become a running joke in the family because I had been debating titles for two months straight already. At one point, it became so bad that my sister declared a three-day moratorium on discussing this topic with her at all. "Tell me again what your book is *really* about?" my parents ask.

My mind flashes back to a few months ago when my father had emergency surgery for a life-threatening situation. He and my stepmom had been stuck in the waiting room of the ER for four hours before even seeing a doctor, by which point his condition had become quite precarious. This took place only weeks after my father had suffered a minor stroke, from which he was still recovering. Yet when I saw them in the hospital two days after the surgery, they were in surprisingly good spirits. Rather than focusing on the unfortunate circumstances they endured in the ER, or the fact that this was the second time in just over a month that they had been in the hospital, they spent the day talking about how wonderful the nurses were, and expressing their gratitude to each nurse who came into the room. In the weeks after this event, my father was diagnosed with a treatable form of cancer. Yet again, his mood remains upbeat. He goes for regular walks up their huge neighborhood hill and exercises at the gym in between treatments whenever he has the energy, which seems often. He listens passionately to classical music, goes for strolls with his beloved dog, writes letters to the editor about important political topics, spends meaningful time with my stepmom, and tells me that he rather likes not having much hair because it makes life simpler. Like many of us (including me), my dad is a natural worrier and tends to get anxious about things he can't control. Yet, despite the intense worries and fears that surface, that could easily spiral him—and sometimes do—he doesn't let those keep him trapped in a world of fear and negativity. Instead, he has found a way to embrace life, with amazing courage, a sense of humor, gratitude, and an open heart.

My father's resilience is an inspiring reminder to me that despite the external challenges we face in our lives, and the internal obstacles we face within our own minds (such as our innate tendency to focus on the negatives, get pulled into fear, and become stuck in unhelpful ruminations), we can learn to embrace the whole of our lives nonetheless. Yes, I think I will stick with my latest title: *Dancing on the Tightrope: Transcending the Habits of Your Mind and Awakening to Your Fullest Life*. This is the message I want to share.

This business of being human is no easy matter. Ask anyone who has lived on this planet for a short while. I recently saw an amazing performance by a juggler on a tightrope gracefully catching and juggling multiple balls in midair. This human life—at least as I know it—is not like that. We don't know which balls will be thrown at us at any given moment. We often lose our balance, we drop the balls, sometimes we fall, and perhaps we even berate ourselves because we feel we *should* be able to balance perfectly on that tightrope. And, when we do find ourselves in moments of balance, we may spend more time than not worrying about when we will lose our balance again.

The "balls" that are thrown at us might be day-to-day stressors and challenges; the unexpected obstacles and traffic jams that detour us, deadlines, all the things that we need to "accomplish" in the day, balancing work, family and kids, paying bills, answering emails, and attempting to find time for ourselves. In addition, we often wrestle with bigger issues, such as relationship challenges, self-doubt, feelings of unworthiness, loss, heartbreaks, change and transition, aging parents, illness, anxiety, depression, our own imperfections, and fears and uncertainty about our future. There is often no clear path through these difficulties, and we frequently go through them without much guidance. Sometimes it feels that we go at it alone.

Neuropsychologist Rick Hanson (Hanson, 2014) says that our lives are greatly shaped by three things: First are the vulnerabilities that we have—often things we come into the world with, such as our temperament and genetic make-up. Second are the challenges that we face in our lives. Third are the resources that we have to handle those challenges. As a clinical psychologist, I am most interested in this third area, and specifically in helping people grow inner resources to meet whatever challenges they may face in their lives with greater resilience. We may not always be able to choose how many balls we have to juggle at a time or how thin the rope is that we have to stand on, but we can learn ways to find longer moments of balance and create safety nets for when we inevitably fall so it will be easier to get back up again. And we can even learn to dance on that tightrope, knowing full well we will fall time and again.

This book will show you how to create a more full and meaningful life, in line with who you most want to be, while accepting your human imperfections and the uncertainties in your life. It will help you to understand five universal, evolutionary challenges—or "habits of the mind"—that we all face as human beings, (in addition to our *personal* stressors), that can take us away from our lives, add to our stress and suffering, and trap us in cycles of negativity. You will learn five specific tools and "antidotes" to work with these habits of the mind, that you can use to enrich your life, reduce your stress, and experience greater joy. The tools in this book will enable you to grow inner resources to become more resilient in the face of whatever stressors and challenges you are dealing with in your life. And you will learn how to become more present, self-compassionate, and aware, so that you can experience the fullness that life has to offer, while coming home to your own open heart.

Over the years, much of my learning to help people grow these inner resources has been on and near the therapy couch. I have spent time on therapy couches myself, as the "patient," finding ways to manage my own stress and anxiety (for better or worse I am wired as a classic "Type A" person and a natural worrier). When I give talks on stress, I often share that I consider myself an expert on the topic mostly because I'm really good at feeling it myself. In addition, I've sought help with larger "balls," such as coping with the profound loss and grief from my mother's death when I was a teenager. I've also learned a tremendous amount about growth and inner resources from my hundreds of patients over the years, who have taught me immeasurable lessons about the strength and resilience of the human spirit. In addition, the exploding field of neuroscience, as well as the research on evidence-based practices in psychology, have provided me invaluable information to help my patients learn the tools to make significant changes in their lives. I share some of these tools with you in this book.

In my previous book, *The Transformative Power of Ten Minutes: An Eight Week Guide to Reducing Stress and Cultivating Well-Being*, I outlined a step-by-step path to reduce stress and increase well-being through specific exercises that take ten minutes or less to complete over the course of one's day. This book might be considered both a prequel and a sequel to *The Transformative Power of Ten Minutes*. It is a stand-alone guide to living a meaningful life, but it also may be used alongside *The Transformative Power of Ten Minutes* to enhance and practice more deeply the tools that are suggested. While my first book is designed to be carried out in small doses, this book can be read in one or more sittings as you choose. The messages, lessons and inspirations are based on my personal experience, my professional experience as a clinical psychologist, my personal practice with mindfulness and my experience using mindfulness with my patients, as well as my quest to understand modern neuroscience, the workings of the brain, and what research has to say on how we can change behavior.

My Own Path

A few months before I started writing this book, I read a book by Dr. Robert Brooks, a beloved mentor from my psychology internship, entitled *Reflections on Mortality: Insights into Meaningful Living*. In the first chapter, Dr. Brooks writes about reflecting on his own life and what led him to where he is today by sharing the perspective of "connecting the dots backwards"—a concept that the late Steve Jobs spoke about in a talk he gave in 2005. It is the notion that only when we look back on our life can we connect the dots and make sense of the path we have chosen.

Reading this prompted me to start connecting the dots back in my own life, and I realized something interesting about mindfulness—which is now an exploding topic of study and practice within the psychology field. Mindfulness practices originated from ancient Buddhist traditions, but were adapted in the Western world by contemporary teachers, such as Jon Kabat-Zinn. I will talk about mindfulness in more detail later, but as Jon Kabat-Zinn explains, mindfulness is a particular way of paying attention. It is, as he defines it, "paying attention in a particular way: on purpose, in the present moment, and nonjudgmentally" (Kabat-Zinn, 1994, p. 4). Learning to pay attention more mindfully in our lives is a thread throughout this book.

Before I knew I wanted to be a psychologist, I wanted to be a writer. I began to write poetry as a child at the age of six. Poetry became a way for me to pay attention to what I was feeling inside, and to capture snapshot moments in my life through words. What I didn't realize until recent years was that for me this was a kind of mindfulness meditation in action—my first experience with mindfulness. It allowed me to be present to whatever was showing up inside.

Now, as I mentioned, I was always type A by nature, pushing myself to achieve, wanting to please, and I had a fair amount of anxiety wired in from birth. But then, on the first day of high school, my whole world came apart when my mother was in a car accident caused by an oncoming driver and died a week later. My mother had been the center of my life for those fifteen years, and the center of our family. She was a loving, devoted mother and selfless woman, who took care of everyone around her, and she provided me with a strong foundation of security and support. Her traumatic loss was devastating to me and my family and a tragedy to all who knew her.

Looking back on this, I realize that this loss led me in two seemingly dichotomous directions in my life. First, it led me to fully embrace the idea of personal control and personal agency, and to ask: how can I do everything in my control to live my life most fully, with the time I have on this planet? How can I take charge of my own well-being and ultimately help others do the same? But the second direction this loss led me in was to ask: How can I learn how to accept my darkest emotions—my fears, sadness, grief, anger—without disconnecting or disowning those parts of myself, and how do I accept the fragility of life—all that I can't control—and somehow find a way to become resilient in the face of this, and help others do the same?

What I realize as I connect the dots backwards is that mindfulness has been helpful for me in both of these ways: bridging this seeming dichotomy of controlling what I can, on one hand, by learning to be fully present each day to life, and on the other hand by accepting what I can't control—and making space to be with difficult emotions while remaining open hearted. Mindfulness has been immensely helpful not only in my own life, but also in the life of my patients, and it is one of the many tools I will be sharing with you in this book.

How This Book Can Be Helpful

One of the reasons I have found mindfulness so helpful in my personal and professional life is that it offers a bridge connecting the mind *and* the body. In our lives, it is so easy for the mind and the body to become disconnected. Sometimes we are stuck in our bodies—in the pain, sadness, anxiety or stress our bodies produce. These sensations can be intense and they can cut us off from the natural flow of our energy and vitality. If we remain stuck in and swept away by the sensations in our bodies, we miss out on the wisdom and perspective that our higher intellect and observing self has to offer. On the other hand, many of us live in our heads and are disconnected from our bodies. We may ignore our body signals; we disconnect from our internal experiences; and we miss out on the richness, information, and wisdom that our bodies offer us. This disconnection, too, can lead to a loss of vitality, energy, and aliveness. With mindfulness and some other practices I will share in this book, we don't just intellectually come to know something, but we also drop into our bodies and notice our inner experiences as felt sensations. We observe what is there, without getting swept away by it. I have seen for my patients, and experienced within myself, tremendous emotional health, harmony, and healing that can come about when there is integration of mind and body.

Opening our hearts and awakening is about embracing the whole of life, and the whole of ourselves. It isn't about learning to balance perfectly on the tightrope (though with practice you may find increasing moments of balance). It's about learning to dance on the tightrope, knowing full well you may lose your balance and fall, and yet be able to get back up again. It's about knowing that sometimes you will be thrown too many balls and sometimes you may lay the balls down altogether, put your hand on your heart, and simply send yourself some compassion. It's about embracing the challenges of being human and growing the inner resources to find the richness and well-being that awaits. It's about learning to relate to life's stressors and challenges so that they don't knock you down for the count, or take you away from the joy and peace that is possible.

Here are a few of the many things that I hope you will learn from this book:

1. This business of being human—and the challenges that go along with it—are probably more common than you think. You are not alone.

2. There are five core evolutionary challenges (habits of our minds) that we all face as human beings that can take us away from living our lives most fully.

3. When we understand these habits and work with them, we grow lasting inner resources to face whatever life may bring our way.

4. You are not crazy, defective, or broken—but you might be lacking some tools that can help you experience life more fully.

5. Well-being is a skill that can be taught, and one that needs to be practiced.

6. There are easy to learn tools that can help you become more resilient in the face of stressors, and that can help you live each day more fully. This book will teach you those tools.

Many years ago, I was driving around an unfamiliar neighborhood trying to look at houses in a town that my father and stepmom were considering for a move. I was with my brother, driving quite slowly on an empty street, when a telephone pole sideswiped my car. At least that's how it seemed at the time. The truth is obviously that I wasn't paying attention to the road, and drove right up against the pole without even knowing it was there, to the tune of two thousand dollars in damage to my car. While fortunately, this was a relatively minor accident and no one was hurt, it was a real wake-up call for me to pay more attention!

Thankfully, we don't have to wait until we drive into a pole to begin to wake up. This book will show you many ways to begin to wake up and pay attention, so that you can embrace your life that awaits.

⌒

In order to make this book more effective in bringing about actual change in your life, I have included brief opportunities to write and reflect in each chapter, so that this material becomes relevant to your own life in a direct way.

To begin this journey:

~ Take a moment and write down some of the current stressors and challenges you are facing in your life. You might divide these into big and small stressors, to distinguish between them.

Please note that while this book will offer you tools and resources to enrich your life no matter what your personal circumstances, if you are dealing with significant challenges (for example a recent trauma or chronic illness or depression), I strongly recommend seeking the guidance of a licensed mental health professional to support your journey toward healing and wholeness. I speak not only as a clinician when I say this, but from the patient side as well, knowing how helpful therapy has been in my own life. This book is for educational purposes only and is not a substitute for treatment.

~ Note your typical responses to these stressors. For example, if you have a challenging boss at work, you might note that you tend to get irritable much of the day in anticipation of working with him/her. If you struggle getting your children up and out of the house every morning, you might note that you tend to say to yourself "Here we go again!" at the start of the day. Make particular note of the kinds of things you say to yourself as you go through your day dealing with your day-to-day challenges.

~ Take a moment to think about the inner resources that you already use in your life to help you. Name them and note how effective they are for you.

~ Now think about what changes you would like to make in your life. If you were living your life to the fullest, how might you show up each day? If you could experience greater well-being in your life, what would you be doing differently?

CHAPTER ONE

Five Habits of the Mind and Why It Matters

(Or: It's Hard to Find Happiness When a Raccoon is Loose in Your House)

T HE WEEK I WAS FINISHING this manuscript, we had a raccoon problem. It started when my son pulled into our driveway one night and noticed eight raccoons gathered by the side of our house, many of them babies. The next night, we accidentally forgot to close the garage door, only to wake up the next morning to a complete disaster in our garage!

The raccoons had pulled apart all the shelves that lined the walls to find every scrap of food we had stored there. Every box that once sat on a shelf was now torn apart and the contents thrown all over the floor. (They especially seemed to like the energy bars.) The following night, I hung a big sign in the kitchen saying "Make Sure to Close the Garage Door!" Thinking we had solved the problem, I was preparing to go to bed and sleep peacefully that night when my husband and I heard a strange scratching, pawing, and banging at the door of the garage that leads into our house. The little rascal had somehow gotten back into the garage and was trapped inside! My husband ran around to the outside of our garage and opened the door, freeing the raccoon.

Afterwards, she sat on our front walkway for several minutes and I got a good look at her. This primitive yet resourceful creature that had wreaked havoc in our garage was actually quite cute. And I realized, she was just doing what nature intended, following her innate, survival instincts to get food for herself and her family. Nonetheless, I was happy to have her return to her natural environment where she no longer needed to make such a mess of things.

Like the raccoon, some of our behaviors are driven by instinctual programs that at one time helped us survive, but unlike the raccoon, are no longer as critical for our survival today. Yet without being aware of it, we often operate throughout our lives from these old, primitive programs. In fact, they may run the show more than we realize. Wired into our brains over millions of years of evolution to help our ancestors survive harsh conditions, these programs that once played a crucial role in the survival of our species have become like habits of our minds that, in many ways, no longer serve us. In fact, they can often make our modern day challenges and stressors *more* difficult to handle.

While these more primitive systems of our brain have been integrated in complex ways with our more recently evolved brain systems, there are ways in which—metaphorically speaking—they haven't been fully upgraded to meet the challenges of our modern lives. We can become trapped in these old programs without realizing it, and they can show up often in our modern lives in sneaky ways, such as undue stress, distraction, anxiety, fear, unhelpful ruminations, self-criticism, negativity and distorted thinking, to name a few. Unknowingly operating from these old, automatic programs can spiral us downward and close us off from the joy, growth, peace, well-being and healing that is possible for us. Once we learn to understand and navigate these innate default patterns, we can free ourselves and open our lives to wider possibilities.

The good news here is that evolution has also hardwired into our brains all the tools that we need to experience greater well-being and resilience. We just need to know how to activate these tools and use them most effectively. Of course, I am simplifying the brain science here, but as we learn to fully integrate these various parts of our brain and develop greater awareness and flexibility, we create more options to build the lives we want.

At times our minds are like that rambunctious raccoon, defaulting to old, innate programs for survival. If left unaware, our minds can run amok and trap us in unhelpful ways that keep us stuck. When we practice the tools in this book, we free ourselves from these automatic, reactive patterns and discover the full potential of who we are.

We will first explore five habits of the mind—or "core evolutionary challenges," as I refer to them going forward—that we face; and subsequently, in the remainder of the book, we will learn tools and antidotes to help us cultivate well-being and resilience.

Challenge #1: The False Alarm

Imagine that the smoke alarm goes off in your house, only there is no real fire. When you investigate more closely, you realize that someone has just burned a piece of toast. Of course, the smoke alarm doesn't know that. It is wired to go off as soon as it detects smoke of any kind. It can't differentiate a false alarm from a life-threatening emergency. Now imagine that the smoke alarm is going off throughout much of the day because a lot of toast is burning in your house, day in and day out. That's a lot of wear and tear on the system and on you, trying to respond to each false alarm.

So herein lies our first evolutionary challenge. We have such an alarm wired into our brains, and it operates in a manner similar to the smoke detector. Our primitive brains developed an alarm system to respond to external, physical threats to our well-being back in ancient times, when we lived on the savannahs and in caves, when we had to deal with predators, such as lions and other wild animals. Those early people who could fight back, or flee quickly, or in some cases freeze (play dead) were the ones who survived to pass on their genes. That's lucky for us, because I wouldn't be writing this and you wouldn't be reading this if it had worked out otherwise. But this fight or flight response—in which our blood pressure rises, heart rate increases, blood flow increases to the fighting muscles and diminishes for less critical functions such as digestion and immune functioning, and stress chemicals such as cortisol and adrenaline are released into our bloodstream—is not necessarily appropriate for many of the challenges that we face in the modern world.

The kinds of threats most of us face are much more internal and psychological in nature: we may sense a threat when someone criticizes us; when we have too many bills to pay or too much to do and not enough time; when we feel unworthy; when our kids aren't listening to us; when we have a test to take; or when we fear others will judge us. Yet as soon as that primitive part of our brain *perceives* a threat, our fight-or-flight response jumps into action. It doesn't know that there is no life-threatening emergency. It prepares our body as if there were one. Now, we may not experience a full blown fight-or-flight response. But we may experience chronic, low grade stress that keeps us in a heightened state of alert and unease, releases stress chemicals into our bloodstream, and over time if unchecked, can create a lot of wear and tear on us both emotionally and physically. In addition, the fight-or-flight response short-circuits our higher thinking brain, so to speak, making it more difficult to respond skillfully to the challenges that we are facing (Goleman, 1995).

The problem is that fighting, fleeing or freezing can't help most of the challenges that we face in our modern day lives. In fact, when we are in fight-or-flight mode, we experience a kind of tunnel vision in which it is harder to step back and see the bigger picture, the wider perspective, and we have less access to resources for coping. We are not fully integrated with our higher thinking brain, because it has gone temporarily "offline" so to speak. If I'm being chased by a lion, I want tunnel vision because the only thing I want to focus on is getting the heck out of there! I don't want my brain to pause in that moment and think of more creative solutions or to stop and send compassion to me for my predicament. But for the modern-day challenges that I face in my daily life, that ability to pause and see the bigger picture could be immensely helpful.

There are a few important points about the false alarm. It is a normal, adaptive response to an external, physical threat, and something that is still essential for our survival and functioning. In and of itself, it is not a "bad" thing, and in fact, we can learn to understand it and make friends with it. As we will see later on, when we learn to work with our false alarm in more skillful ways, it can become a helpful signal that gives us important information. As psychiatrist Daniel Siegel points out, we can learn how to consciously harness the powers of our more recently evolved brain systems in order to calm our innate fear response (Siegel, 2010).

The problem comes when we are so accustomed to our stress response that we think it is normal to be chronically stressed, when we ignore these signals altogether and don't even notice them anymore, or when we can't shut it off. Short term, our stress response can mobilize us, energize us, and motivate us to perform optimally. It can be helpful and adaptive. But we need to know how to work with it, not against it. Long term, chronic activation of our stress response can drain and deplete us. Our fight-or-flight response is designed to turn off and go back to baseline when the immediate threat has passed. The problem today is that we may keep our stress response activated simply because of our own thinking—for example, ruminating about something that upset us in the past, or something that *might* happen in the future—even when there is no immediate threat in front of us. When chronically activated, we don't experience that "reset" that nature intended.

> *When we learn to work with the "false alarm," we create a felt sense of safety and an anchor of stability amidst the storms. From this place, we can respond more skillfully to the challenges we face.*

The Many Faces of the False Alarm

Let's look at some of the many aspects of the false alarm, and how it might play a role in our lives, knowingly or unknowingly.

Jake is a computer analyst at a start-up company. His job requires him to work long hours, and this doesn't leave him much time for himself. When he wakes up, he typically feels a sense of tension and unease thinking about the day ahead, the long commute, and all that he has to do. Because he is often exhausted, he sleeps until the last possible minute, but then white knuckles his commute through heavy traffic, swearing and griping along the way, and often barely makes it to the office on time. When he walks through the door at work, his stress level is already high, and he finds himself more irritable with coworkers than he wants to be. He also finds himself flying off the handle easily when people question him or look at him the wrong way. By the time he gets home, he is wiped out and tends to "crash" in front of the TV with a few beers to try and chill out before starting the cycle all over again the next day. At Jake's most recent annual physical, his doctor noted that he had put on weight and that his blood pressure was high.

Aisha works full time and is the mother of three children. As much as she loves her children she finds that her teens especially challenge her. They try her patience and, despite her intentions, she often finds herself yelling and screaming at them. When Aisha's teens won't listen to her, or when they roll their eyes or forget to do the things she asks, it's as if the alarm bells go off signaling a predator is attacking. Her emotions escalate quickly and then she often feels badly afterwards for flying off the handle. Often, Aisha feels frazzled and drained throughout the day. After arriving at work she has very little time to rest and replenish, leaving her on edge and sometimes depleted. She feels like she should be enjoying her life, because she has much that is stable and good in it, but more often than not she finds herself overly stressed.

Serika is a college student in the midst of her senior year. In addition to the challenges of attending a competitive school with intense courses and a heavy workload, she experiences a great deal of anxiety. The source of some of this is external, from the outside demands of her university, but much of it is internal, from pressure she puts on herself to excel and earn all A's. She knows she should eat healthier and sleep more, but she has difficulty sticking to this plan. Recently, she has begun suffering from panic attacks, unexplained stomach pains with no known medical cause, and insomnia.

Sergio is a young man is his late twenties. He has experienced mild anxiety throughout his life, but this has worsened recently and has begun to interfere with his life. He finds himself going out less to avoid the social anxiety he experiences in crowds. He finds new situations threatening and steers clear of them, even though they might involve things he would enjoy doing. He also finds himself procrastinating frequently and "freezing" when he faces deadlines, waiting until the last possible moment to complete projects, which creates additional stress for him.

～

~ Take a moment and reflect on any ways that the false alarm shows up in your life. Take a few minutes to write this down.

~ Think about the kind of situations that trigger your stress response. Is there a pattern? How do you react when you perceive a threat? Do you tend to fight (e.g., yell argue, get angry, explode), flee (e.g., avoid or ignore the problem, procrastinate), or freeze (e.g., shut down, isolate, become overwhelmed and seemingly paralyzed)?

~ When do you tend to get anxious, and how do you typically react when you feel this way? Is your reaction helpful or unhelpful to the situation?

~ What tools do you currently have in your repertoire to help you when your stress response is in high gear?

~ Do you notice when your stress response gets turned on, or are you so used to it that it just feels like the norm?

~ Do you have ways to "reset" throughout the day?

Challenge #2: A Dial Stuck in an Unhelpful Place

Imagine that there is a dial that controls the brain's attention system. One of the settings of this dial is "fully attentive and present to what is happening in the moment." Another setting is "mind-wandering." Some of the "mind-wandering" state involves creative, conscious daydreaming that can be helpful and important, but much of it involves the mind being lost in thought about the past, the future, and self-referential thoughts that have an unhelpful, ruminative quality and correlate with negative mood states, unhappiness, anxiety and depressive thinking. Now imagine that the dial is stuck in the mind-wandering state much of the time, especially the more unhelpful kind of mind-wandering.

Herein lies our second evolutionary challenge:

When our brains are not focused on a specific task at hand, they are often in this mind-wandering state. In fact, one study (Killingsworth and Gilbert, 2010) estimates that when not focused on a specific task, we are in this mind-wandering state about fifty percent of the time. That's a lot of time in our lives spent in mind-wandering—with much of it the unhelpful, unconscious kind of rumination.

There is a name for the regions of the brain that are active during this kind of mind-wandering. Scientists refer to it as the "default mode network" of the brain. While these regions of our brain are still not fully understood, it is believed that there was an evolutionary purpose for this network. Back in our ancestors' time, this part of the brain may have helped early humans reflect on past behavior in order to plan for future actions (MacKinnon, 2017). However, in modern times, this kind of mind-wandering that our brains default to doesn't always serve us so well. In fact, when we are engaged in unconscious, ruminative mind-wandering, it can take us away from experiencing the here and now of our lives.

Neuropsychologist Rick Hanson describes that our brains are wired to play simulations of past events and imagined future ones over and over, like clips of a movie, even when doing so no longer serves us and adds to our "suffering" (Hanson & Mendius, 2009). As psychiatrist Daniel Siegel explains (2017), studies have shown that the ruminative kind of mind-wandering can actually cause us to be unhappy, and the opposite state—being in a state of presence—can lead to an increased experience of happiness.

Automatic Pilot

When our minds are somewhere else, we are not present to what is happening here and now. That means that we are missing out on what is here, in this present moment, which is really the only moment we have. Yet, many of us operate from this automatic-pilot mode of being much of the time. We are caught up in our own thoughts more than we realize, and we don't notice what is in front of us. We go through the motions of our day, missing some of the best moments available to us. We drive in our cars and miss the sights; we take a shower and miss the sensation of the warm water and the aroma of the shampoo; we eat our food but miss savoring the flavors and textures; we have conversations but sometimes only half pay attention—all because our minds are somewhere else.

⌒

Think about a time when you felt fully alive. Perhaps it was an experience in nature, or a moment of connection with someone you care about, enjoying a magnificent meal, or zip-lining in the woods. Chances are, your mind was not wandering, ruminating, or lost in thought at that time. Now think about how much of the time you are fully present during your day. For most of us, it isn't that often.

~ Name a few times when you were fully present to what was happening in the moment as it was unfolding. What were you doing? What was the experience like for you?

~ Name a few recent times when you were on automatic pilot, and/or when you were caught up in mind-wandering. What were you doing? What do you think you missed because of this?

When we learn to work with the "stuck dial," we experience greater presence, and the authentic happiness that accompanies this.

The Many Faces of a Stuck Dial

Derick has been waiting for seven months to finally have a vacation. During his day-to-day life he finds his mind wandering much of the time from one topic to another, and he is often lost in thoughts and ruminations that keep him stuck in his head. He views his vacation as a chance to get away from this constant mind chatter. However, when he is finally on the beach, he finds himself wondering for long periods of time where to go for dinner that night. When he is walking along the beach, he gets caught in thoughts about how his boss is going to respond to a new proposal he will share when he gets back. When he is sitting at dinner with his family, his mind is caught in thoughts about the new book he bought and when he will be able to start reading it. Much of the time, he doesn't even recognize he is doing this.

Maria works as a human resources director. She has many friends outside of work whom she spends time with on the weekends. While she has a job that she enjoys and friends whom she cares for, her mind wanders into the past much of the time, and this takes her attention away from the things in front of her. Maria had a difficult childhood and experienced emotional abuse as a child. Even though she was in therapy in early adulthood to help her work through this, she still finds her mind frequently thinking about things that happened in her past. At work, she often finds herself lost in ruminations and realizes that ten minutes or more might have elapsed in which she drifted away from the task at hand, lost in thought about something that happened long ago. On weekends, she might be sitting around with a group of friends and find her mind wandering into the past, often bringing with it old feelings of inadequacy and self-doubt. Even though she is with supportive people, her ruminations can often bring about a depressed mood as she relives the past and becomes quiet and disengaged.

Jane, a young woman in her mid-twenties, goes through her day rarely in the present moment. Here is an example of a typical day: When she brushes her teeth she thinks about what she will pack for lunch. When she packs her lunch she thinks about how bad the traffic will be on the way to work. When she drives to work, she plays out possible scenes of things that might go wrong throughout the day. When she is at work she thinks about how she can't wait to be home. When she is home, she thinks about what the next day will be like at work—how much traffic there will be, who will annoy her, what meetings she has, and so on.

Challenge #3: The Noisy Person at the Movie Theater

Imagine sitting in a movie theater, excited to immerse yourself in a great movie that you've been looking forward to watching for quite some time. Some noisy person sits down next to you and as soon as the movie begins, he starts a running commentary on the film. : "Can you believe what she just did there— that's crazy…Oh my God that was so stupid of her…I can tell you where this is going and it's not going to be good…I can't believe he did that—what is wrong with him? This is a disaster!" Here you are, just trying to enjoy your movie, and you've got this constant running narrative taking you away from what is happening, and putting a damper on your experience.

Well, I'm not sure if you've noticed, but for many of us, it is as if we have this constant narrator in our own heads. So not only do we have a tendency for our minds to wander and ruminate, but very often we attach judgments and interpretations to our internal discourse. If you start to pay attention, you will likely notice that we humans talk to ourselves throughout the day, and much of what we say isn't necessarily accurate or helpful. In fact, it can be quite critical and negative.

So herein lies our third evolutionary challenge. This one will stretch your mind a bit, and it doesn't completely follow the pattern of the other challenges, but bear with me and I think you'll see what I'm talking about. The challenge I am referring to has to do with the evolution of language.

Wait a minute, you might say. How can language, which is an advanced cognitive capacity of our brains, not a primitive one, be a challenge in any way? Language has helped us to evolve as a species and create civilization as we know it today, in all its glory. The capacity for language has facilitated some of the greatest inventions and creations, from science to the arts. Yet there is a down side that we may not recognize. Instead of just experiencing things directly through our senses (as babies do before language develops), we often have a running commentary, a narrative, an interpretation of what is happening, a cognitive lens through which we look, a story that gets attached to our experience.

For example, we don't just experience loss from losing a job. We might also tell ourselves that we are a failure because of it. If we experience a break up of a relationship, we might not only feel the pain of the breakup, but also attach to that experience our own narrative that we must not be good enough, or that nothing will ever work out for us. I don't imagine that the squirrel outside my window is telling himself that he is a loser for not making friends with a new squirrel in the neighborhood, or telling himself that he isn't going to amount to anything because he didn't collect enough acorns this week. Yet we humans do this sort of thing often.

So not only do we have a direct experience of an event in our lives, but we also attach a story to it. Health psychologist Kelly McGonigal (2017) describes this constant inner dialogue as another aspect of the default mode of the brain, along with the tendency to engage in mind-wandering previously described. She suggests that this kind of mental process may have helped our ancestors survive (by constantly focusing on what is wrong and what can be improved), but it doesn't serve us as well today. The way that we use language and thought to narrate our experience and provide constant running commentary can lead to distraction and dissatisfaction, and can create suffering and unhappiness for us (McGonigal, 2017).

If we stop and pay attention to the things we say to ourselves, we will recognize that they are often critical, unhelpful, inaccurate, distorted, and just not true. We berate ourselves when we make mistakes. We turn minor situations into catastrophes in our mind. We assume others are thinking badly of us, even when there is no evidence to support this. We misread situations. We personalize loss and make it about something we are lacking, or we assume responsibility and blame for bad things that happened that are out of our control. There is a whole field in psychology called Cognitive-Behavioral Therapy, which looks at the distorted thought traps that we commonly experience and how these thoughts contribute to negative mood states, such as anxiety and depression.

As if that isn't enough, another problem with language is that we often take our thoughts as reality, and not just as the passing mental events that they are. The field of Acceptance and Commitment Therapy (ACT) has a lot to say about how language traps us in this way, and how it can contribute to our suffering (Hayes and Smith, 2005).

Consider this example: Jessica finds herself looking at an online invitation she just received for a party and says the following words to herself: "I want to go to that party, but I'm way too anxious." By saying those words, she fuses her thoughts, emotions and behaviors into one, making a very convincing argument to herself that her thoughts and emotions actually prevent her from getting in her car and driving to the party. If I think I can't do something, then it must be so. If I think I'm a loser then it must be so. These are some of the traps in which language ensnares us.

When we learn to work with "the noisy person at the movie theater," we develop the capacity for greater perspective and self-compassion.

The Many Faces of the Noisy Person at the Movie Theater

Let's explore some examples of how language, and the narratives we construct, can contribute to our suffering.

Andre was a perfectionist with one particular fault: he couldn't accept when he made mistakes. Unfortunately in his line of work in which he had to do meticulous data entry, mistakes were commonplace. Whenever Andre made a mistake that was caught by a supervisor, he would beat himself up repeatedly for what happened. It didn't matter that his supervisor wasn't upset by it. The story that Andre told himself is that he screwed up once again, could never get it right, and was probably going to lose his job. Andre would replay the mistake over and over in his mind, and he would call himself an "idiot" or "stupid." These mental reruns came out especially at night when he was trying to fall asleep. Replaying the scene of the mistake over and over in his mind, he would mentally berate himself, making it difficult to fall asleep. He also did this in social situations when he didn't explain something as clearly as he would like, or when he thought he said something that others would perceive as "stupid." The stories he attached to these moments were extreme and didn't fit the circumstances, yet he played them just the same, leaving him filled with self-doubt and insecurity.

Randy injured his back six months earlier and despite surgery, continued to experience some back pain. Even before he got out of bed in the morning, he would think about what his pain level was going to be and predict that it was going to be a bad day. After getting up and feeling some sensation in his back, his mind immediately jumped to thoughts such as "Oh God, how am I going to get through the day?" and "This is gonna be another doozy." In addition, his mind frequently jumped to extremes, such as "I'll never be able to do what I want" and "This has ruined me," even though he had returned to working, socializing, and doing light exercise. He was unaware of how much these thoughts caused his muscles to contract and constrict, and his mood to plummet.

Margo was an intelligent, driven and hard-working woman, who was highly successful in her profession. However, she often had a difficult time relaxing, and she put pressure on herself that was essentially self-imposed. On her days off, she felt that she needed to be busy constantly and when she sat down for a few minutes she often told herself that she was being "lazy" and there was a lot that she should get done. She watched the clock often and told herself "I've got to drop this off now; I've got to get to the bank…" and would feel pressured if something delayed her, even though she had more than enough time to do these things. When someone suggested that she might benefit from meditation, she told herself "I could never do that! I'm not cut out to sit still!"

~

~ Notice the narrator in your own head as you go about your day. What things do you tend to say to yourself? Are they accurate and true? Are they helpful or unhelpful? Do they make difficult situations worse, or easier to bear?

~ Is the voice of your narrator self-critical, or self-compassionate?

~ How does your narrator affect what you do or don't do in your life? Are there ways that this voice stops you from doing things that you might otherwise want to do?

Challenge #4: The Finger Trap Dilemma

Have you ever seen one of those gag toys used to play a practical joke on people, where you insert an index finger of each hand into a small cylinder contraption woven from bamboo? Once you insert your fingers, they become trapped. The trick is that the harder you pull to get them out, the more stuck they become. The way to be freed is to do something counterintuitive (spoiler alert): push the fingers farther inside the trap, towards one another, to loosen the trap and be released.

This may be a silly toy, but what does any of this have to do with our own lives? The Finger Trap Dilemma is actually a common metaphor used in Acceptance and Commitment Therapy (ACT) to illustrate an important point about our lives and what causes us to suffer. We can easily fall victim to a similar kind of trap in our own mind, and it can affect our lives in profound ways.

Welcome to the fourth evolutionary challenge. As a species, we evolved to seek pleasure and avoid pain. That was a good thing for our ancestors because the kind of painful experiences that they most needed to avoid to survive were external physical threats, such as dangerous animals and poisonous plants. This strategy of avoidance made a lot of sense at the time because it helped to solve a serious problem: if I avoid this unpleasant and dangerous snake right now, I will not be bitten and die.

However, our brains operate from that same principle in our modern lives more than we may realize, except the kind of pain we tend to avoid is much more internal in nature: our own uncomfortable body sensations, thoughts and emotions. The paradox is that the attempted "solution"—to push these internal experiences away—does not solve a problem. It creates one. When we experience uncomfortable feelings, like boredom, sadness, grief, anger, fear, or physical discomforts, our human tendency is to push these feelings away, to avoid them at all cost. The field of Acceptance and Commitment Therapy calls this "experiential avoidance" (Hayes and Smith, 2005). The trap is that often the more we try to push these unpleasant feelings away, the more they keep us from living the life that might be most meaningful to us.

For example, if we distract ourselves from our emotional discomfort by surfing the web and playing video games because we don't think we're good enough to go after that new opportunity awaiting, we let those limiting beliefs stop us and never take the steps that would help us create more meaning in our lives. If we do everything we can to avoid feeling anxiety, we might also avoid those very activities and interactions that enrich our lives. If we push away our grief and sadness, we deprive ourselves of the healing that comes with turning towards these dark emotions, and we might isolate ourselves from meaningful connections in the process.

The way out of this dilemma is to do what is counterintuitive: lean into the discomfort. We certainly aren't taught that in school, or through the media messages that bombard us with quick fixes or the advertisements that promise us immediate happiness if we just buy the newest product. We are not taught that our well-being depends on understanding the finger trap dilemma or that learning to lean into emotional discomfort can bring with it opportunities for wholeness and healing.

When we learn to work with the "finger trap dilemma,"
we develop greater trust in our own capacity to bear life's
challenges, accept what is, and embrace the whole of ourselves.

The Many Faces of the Finger Trap Dilemma

There are many ways that we may tend to avoid our internal experiences. Take a look at the following examples and see if you notice yourself in any of them.

When my mother died, I was in the beginning of high school. I had always been a good student, but after her death, I threw myself into my schoolwork even more. I didn't miss a day of school. I didn't ask for any extensions. I was active in clubs and activities. I didn't realize it at the time, but I allowed myself very little space to experience my grief and sadness. In a journal I kept at the time, I wrote to myself how I couldn't understand why I was feeling depressed and instead I should be happy and grateful for all the good things in my life. Sadness was something I tried not to let myself feel. It wasn't until later in my life that I was able to fully mourn my mother's death. The cost of pushing away all that grief was that it showed up in other ways as anxiety.

Fernando moved from the West Coast to Boston when he was offered a great job out of college. Though much of his family remained on the West Coast, he didn't visit them because he was afraid to fly. The anticipated anxiety of being on an airplane was so powerful that it stopped him from doing something that was important to him. He also let his anxiety stop him from doing other things in his life that he feared, such as dating and driving on the highway.

Noelle loved to be busy constantly and didn't do well with down time. In fact, she was addicted to being busy and used it to escape the boredom and monotony of her life. She constantly had her phone in hand when she was away from home and was checking her social media sites, her email, and surfing the Internet non-stop. When she was home, she would often spend hours playing games on her computer to fill her time, and she would sometimes engage in mindless eating. When she wasn't constantly busy, she would feel restless and unhappy, though she never stopped long enough to figure out why this was so. Whenever she experienced something unpleasant, she moved away from it by distracting herself, even though doing so kept her from discovering a deeper and more lasting satisfaction.

~

- ~ What emotions do you most tend to push away or dismiss? What is the cost of doing this?

- ~ What situations do you avoid that you would like to approach but are afraid to because it will be too uncomfortable?

- ~ When you think about the idea of leaning into discomfort, what feelings and sensations arise? What are your first reactions to this concept?

Challenge #5: The Velcro Problem

The final evolutionary challenge that we will explore has to do with a Velcro problem. Yes, you read that right: Velcro, like the kind of fastening strips that things adhere to strongly. As neuroscientist Rick Hanson says, our brains are like Velcro for the negative, and Teflon for the positive experiences (Hanson and Medius, 2009). To understand what this means, imagine that as you go through your day, all the little negative things that happen stick in your brain like Velcro, and all the little positive moments slip right out of your awareness, like the slippery surface of a non-stick Teflon pan. Whether we realize it or not, we are biased to look for and hold onto negative experiences, and to miss, overlook, or dismiss the positive ones—and we have our ancestors to thank for that.

This all made sense in ancient times. Our early ancestors needed to be hypervigilant about the dangers around them in order to survive. As psychologist Ronald Siegel describes (2010), those early people whose brains were able to remember and learn from negative experiences were far better able to survive than those whose brains focused primarily on positive experiences. This "negativity bias," referred to by neuroscientists, was an essential part of our survival as a species. Those less fortunate ancestors with positively-biased brains, who focused on collecting carrots at the expense of avoiding sticks (that could, in fact, be snakes), didn't fare so well in the long run (Hanson, 2013).

Think about how this might play out in your own life. Imagine that you received heartfelt feedback from a friend, romantic partner, or a boss that included both positive feedback regarding all the things this person appreciates about you, and also negative feedback on things they suggested you could change to improve yourself. Now imagine that they had twenty-five things on the positive list, and two things on the negative list. What do you think would stick in your head from that conversation? What might you be thinking about as you fell asleep at night? If you are like most people, you would probably focus on the two negative things that were said.

As another example, imagine a parent with two small children going through their morning routine. For thirty minutes, the children are well behaved and cooperative, and the parent is quietly going about morning preparations, barely noticing the children. Suddenly one of the children grabs or pushes the other, and a minor scuffle breaks out. The parent immediately starts yelling and is upset about their bad behavior (even though the previous thirty minutes of excellent behavior went unacknowledged). That is the negativity bias in action.

When we learn to address the "Velcro problem," we invite gratitude and joy into our lives.

The Many Faces of the Velcro Problem

Let's explore some further examples of how the Velcro problem might show up in your life.

Monique is a woman in her mid-thirties who tends to see the glass as half empty. Here is what she saw as she went through a particular day: Her day began with her alarm not going off, and her husband waking her up a few minutes later. She immediately became focused on the fact that she was five minutes behind her morning routine. Then she noticed her husband left the cap off the toothpaste and the toilet seat up, which intensified her irritability. On the way to work, she was stuck behind the slowest driver on the road, and once she got to work one of her least favorite coworkers decided to carry on a very loud and long conversation in the next cubicle. The cafeteria ran out of her favorite kind of sandwich, and she had to stay an extra fifteen minutes to help a new employee learn the ropes.

Here is what she missed seeing as she went through her day: Her husband was paying attention to her and realized her alarm hadn't gone off, even though he himself was scrambling to get out the door. Knowing she was running late, he had made coffee for her, which she had grabbed on the way out the door. On the drive to work, the azaleas were in full bloom and the lawns were a lush green due to the recent rains. One of her co-workers remembered to ask her how her mother was doing, knowing her mother had been sick last week. At the cafeteria, she tried a new salad that she rather liked. The new employee whom she helped after work was very appreciative of her assistance and clearly benefited from the extra time she took to explain things.

Morgan is a chief officer at a big corporation where she manages hundreds of employees. While she is devoted to the growth and success of her company, she tends to focus mostly on what is going wrong at work rather than on what is going well. Whenever she goes into work, her mind immediately latches on to what wasn't done, who didn't meet the deadlines, who fell short on productivity, who called in sick, and who is not being as efficient as she would like. She is often irritable and short-tempered with others, even though this is not who she wants to be. Her negativity often rubs onto others; she has a reputation for being critical and a person that others should avoid. The morale in the office is impacted because of this.

~

~ How does the Velcro problem show up in your life? In what ways do you tend to notice more negatives than positives in your day?

~ When positive things occur within your day, do you pause and take them in? Do they register on your "radar screen" and do you savor these moments in your day?

~ What factors influence the negativity to positivity ratio in your day? Are there things that you are already doing to help you experience more positivity in your day?

OK, So We Have These Core Challenges—Now What?

It is helpful to recognize that these five evolutionary challenges are ones we all experience. They played a crucial role in our survival as a species and they are normal, adaptive responses to the difficult environment in which our ancestors lived. The brain structures that have become integrated with our more recently evolved brain networks continue to play an important role in our modern day functioning and at times can provide us with vital and beneficial information.

For example, our fight-or-flight response is helpful and necessary when there are real threats to attend to. Creative day-dreaming can be essential for maintaining a healthy brain (Waldman, 2014), and at times we need our minds to wander to the past to help plan for the future. That inner commentator in our heads can guide us in helpful ways when we learn to let our narrator work for us, not against us. There are times when keeping the door closed and avoiding difficult emotions might be a helpful strategy if we are feeling too vulnerable or too overwhelmed to handle something in the moment. And noticing what isn't going well can sometimes help us to improve our current situation.

How These Core Challenges Add to Our Suffering

But it can also be beneficial to understand the ways these five evolutionary challenges contribute to a great deal of suffering for us and can make it harder to experience well being. We already have inevitable day-to-day small stressors, and bigger challenges that we face in our lives: the "balls" that get thrown at us at any given time. But these five evolutionary challenges can exacerbate our day-to-day challenges and make it harder to cope with our lives. Imagine not only juggling balls being thrown at you on the tightrope but wearing a lead vest while you are doing so—and maybe not even realizing that you are wearing the lead vest!

Here is an example to illustrate what I mean:

Jan recently broke up with her romantic partner. This is one of those inevitable life losses, and it is painful in and of itself. There is natural sadness due to this loss. But now, every time Jan meets someone new, she become hypervigilant and anxious, waiting for the next shoe to drop. She is often on "high alert." Even when she thinks about dating or visits a dating website, she experiences this anxiety, and sometimes it is intense (challenge #1—the false alarm). Jan also finds her mind wandering a lot—ruminating about what went wrong in the relationship, and worrying that she will never meet anyone. And even when she is engaging in pleasurable activities, such as a trip to the beach, she finds she is lost in her head and not often present in the moment (challenge #2—the dial stuck in an unhelpful place).

Jan has also been spending a lot of time lately constructing a narrative about how she is a loser, how guys must not like her because she is unattractive and unworthy, and how no one will ever want to be with her (challenge #3—the noisy person at the movie theater). When feelings of sadness come up around the loss, she distracts herself with alcohol or eating, and she avoids opportunities to go out with others for fear of potential sadness, or the anxiety described above (challenge #4—the finger trap dilemma). She looks through the world with clouded glasses—focusing more on what's wrong than on what's right about herself and her life (challenge # 5—the Velcro problem).

As you can see from this example, these challenges often do not operate in isolation; they can interact with one another and feed off one another in cumulative ways.

The Continuum

One way to understand these challenges is to think about them on a kind of continuum, where at one end of the continuum these challenges play a minor role in our lives and on the other end of the continuum, they play a large role in our lives and may even be the source of great psychological distress. If we have an active or over-active fight-or-flight response, we might experience a great deal of stress, anxiety or even panic. If we spend excessive amounts of time engaged in ruminations and maladaptive thinking, we may experience depression. If we are at the extreme end of engaging in avoidant behaviors to keep our painful emotions at bay, we might struggle with addictions or anxiety that stops us from living our lives. But even on the mild end of the continuum, these core challenges can sneak up on us unaware, and take us away from experiencing well-being.

~

~ Which one (or more) of these five challenges is your biggest personal challenge?

~ Which one(s) gets in the way most of who you want to be?

Understanding these five core challenges can help you identify your particular vulnerabilities. While our brains are wired to experience all five challenges, there may be one or more that are especially troublesome for you. For myself, I tend to struggle most with the false alarm going off when there is no real fire. I now know this about myself, and I can see how my personal experiences and day-to-day stressors interface with this tendency for my brain to perceive danger. Knowing this helps me to remind myself that there are no bears chasing me when I find myself triggered, such as when I am stuck in traffic on my way to work, or when a situation doesn't work out as planned. Some of my patients tend to get stuck in negativity;

others get caught up in ruminations that contribute to unhappiness and sometimes depression. When we understand the working of our brains, we can begin to step out of these automatic, often primitive responses. We can learn antidotes and grow inner resources that help us to create new and more helpful responses.

The remainder of this book will teach you tools to do this. The five tools that you will learn will become your toolkit, to provide antidotes to these evolutionary challenges and to offer resources to face whatever personal challenges are present in your life. These tools will not stop the appearance of these evolutionary challenges (remember we are all human!), but they will assist you to recognize when they are present and when you are caught in unhelpful, reactive patterns, and they will offer beneficial strategies and practices to pursue that will help you to improve your life.

Seeing the Glass Half Full

Importantly, becoming aware of our evolutionary challenges can remind us that we are human and that we are all in good company. We can remind ourselves that all the core challenges are *not* "bad"— they are healthy, adaptive responses—just not necessarily ones that are adaptive for all of our current circumstances. This can be a reminder to be compassionate with ourselves! In addition, we can learn to see each of these challenges as an *opportunity* that can teach us something about what is most needed in our lives to be fully awake and alive, to experience all the richness life has to offer. Reframing it in this way, we can learn to welcome the appearance of all these challenges and use them as reminders to practice skills for well-being and grow inner resources. We will explore this in the chapters ahead.

The Plasticity of Your Brain

Part of the good news that I want to highlight has to do with the plasticity of our brains—an exciting discovery made within the field of neuroscience. No, our brains are not made of plastic, but they do have an amazing ability to change throughout our lives, to form new neural connections, to create new neural pathways, and to reorganize based on our experiences and behaviors. This neuroplasticity means that we are not stuck in our old, automatic ways. Now, if we keep repeating our old, automatic patterns and behaviors that keep us stuck, we will strengthen the circuitry that is already there, reinforcing what isn't working. But, if we practice using new tools that allow us to create new experiences (e.g., calming our false alarms, stepping out of mind-wandering and into the present moment, taking lightly the words of the noisy person at the movie theater, embracing our difficult emotions, and seeing more positives in our day) we use different brain circuitry to wire in new pathways of well-being. As psychiatrist Daniel Siegel explains: "Where attention goes, neural firing flows, and neural connection grows" (Siegel, 2017).

If I want to build the foundation for my new home, I will use many tools to do so: a hammer, a level, a saw, a concrete mixer, and so on. Each tool contributes in its own way to the strong, solid foundation of my home. Once I have this strong foundation built, storms may come—wind, rain, hail—but the home can withstand these storms, and can even be a safe haven for me until the storms pass. Knowing this, it can then also become a place of creativity, peace, discovery, joy and love.

I invite you to learn the five tools that follow, to help you build a strong foundation where you can come home to your fullest self.

CHAPTER TWO

The Flashlight: Using Mindfulness to Help Us Wake Up to Our Lives

M ANY YEARS AGO, when my now grown children were young, I had to have an MRI of my hip. At that time I was working in my outpatient practice, raising two small children, and training for triathlons. I led an extremely busy life and I greatly enjoyed what I was doing, but I felt a lot like that juggler I described at the beginning of the book, except that I was definitely dropping a lot of balls and losing my balance frequently. That day in the MRI machine was quite eye opening for me. I discovered that I loved it in there! I didn't want to come out. Strange as it may sound, there was something freeing about being immobilized in a small space where I couldn't move, or do anything for that matter except follow my breath and listen to the noises around me. Being given permission to "do nothing" and to not "have to" accomplish anything for those thirty minutes was enlightening. It helped me realize how frenetic the pace of my life was, and how beneficial it would be for me to find other moments in my day (besides being in an MRI machine) to slow down and create a space to be present in stillness. It was like being handed a flashlight and suddenly seeing something that I hadn't recognized before. Having that awareness propelled me to make changes and incorporate more small moments in my day to just be and not do.

Tool One: The Flashlight

Imagine that we each had a flashlight that we could carry around with us in our front pocket. Every time we turned it on, we would notice when we were caught up in one of the evolutionary challenges discussed in Chapter One. We would notice when our false alarm was going off, and when that noisy person at the movie theater was starting to talk again. We could catch ourselves when our brains started to tip towards the negative, and we would notice when we were drifting into ruminative thinking yet again. We could catch ourselves when we were getting lost in our heads and simply missing out on what was in front of us right now. We would notice when we started to avoid our own feelings in unhelpful ways. This simple act of noticing could be tremendously powerful in our lives, and could bring us some freedom and choice that we didn't realize was there. Read on to learn how.

While the flashlight can help us in all dimensions of our life, and can help us to notice and work with all five of the evolutionary challenges, this chapter will focus most on how the flashlight can help us to work with the false alarm and the dial stuck in an unhelpful place, in order to: 1) Create a felt sense of safety; 2) Gain greater perspective on whatever challenges we face so we can take skillful action, and 3) Step into the present moment, which is the only moment in which we can truly live.

How Mindfulness Becomes Our Flashlight

Our flashlight is one of our most fundamental and important tools. As I said in *The Transformative Power of Ten Minutes,* we can't change what we don't see. If we walk around in a dark room we will likely stumble and fall on the furniture and other obstacles there. However, if we carry a flashlight with us, the obstacles won't disappear, but we can navigate with more ease. So our flashlight is *awareness,* but it is a particular kind of awareness. It is *mindful awareness,* or *mindfulness.* It is, going back to Jon Kabat-Zinn's (1994) definition of a particular way of paying attention that I mentioned earlier: paying attention, on purpose, in the present moment, without judgment. So with mindfulness, we are observing what is happening with a quality of openness, and curiosity. This kind of awareness is available to all of us, but due to some of the evolutionary challenges of our brain, it is a skill that we need to practice to be able to access and use most effectively.

Let's examine this kind of attention a bit further. There is an intentional quality about it. We are *choosing* to pay attention, to observe whatever is happening *right now,* as compared to mindlessly going through the motions of our day. When we are being mindful, there is an observing quality to our moment-to-moment unfolding experience. We notice what is happening—we observe and accept our body sensations, thoughts and emotions—without judging what we are experiencing as good or bad. If we do find ourselves judging (which our minds love to do), we simply get curious and notice that we are judging, and that awareness allows us a space in which we can soften and even allow in some self-compassion and kindness.

For example, it would not be mindful when I was lying in the MRI machine to be caught up in judgmental thoughts such as, "What's wrong with me? Am I the only person on the planet who views this MRI experience like being at a spa? I must be truly crazy!" and "What's wrong with me that I am so driven that I can't slow down?" That would not be being mindful. However, if while lying there I notice these thoughts and bring some curiosity and acceptance to what I am experiencing, then I am being mindful: "Isn't this interesting. Here I am noticing how relaxed I feel in this forced stillness, and there goes my mind again pulling me away from my experience and getting me tangled up in critical judgments in my head. I can see that happening, and yet I am also aware of the calmness in my body right now."

Do you hear the difference? Those are two very different experiences. One is operating on automatic pilot, and the other snaps me out of automatic pilot as I observe what is happening.

We can practice this kind of mindful awareness informally, as we go through the ordinary events of our day, by simply noticing whatever arises in the present moment, with this quality of attention. When we are being mindful and carrying our flashlight with us, we can notice our thoughts, emotions, and physical sensations with this intentional quality of presence and non-judgment, as we engage fully with *this* moment. Bringing this kind of mindful awareness into our day is the essence of the flashlight, and it is a tool we can carry with us everywhere.

As another example of bringing mindfulness informally into your day, notice the difference between saying to yourself: "I am so anxious" versus "I notice that I am feeling a lot of anxiety in my body right now." Do you hear the observing, non-judgmental voice in the second sentence, and the focus on present moment awareness? Do you see how the feeling of anxiety is noticed as something that comes and goes, as opposed to it being a fixed part of who you are in the first phrase, "I am so anxious"? We can practice bringing this quality of attention to our experiences as we go through our day.

We can also cultivate mindfulness more formally, for example, through sitting meditation. While this formal practice is not the focus in this book, I encourage you to explore it further as it will enhance your ability to use the flashlight. When we practice mindfulness more formally, we bring our attention to some aspect of our present-moment experience, such as our breath, over and over again. One misconception about mindfulness meditation is that if we don't experience calmness and a quieting of our minds, then "it didn't work." With mindfulness (both formal and informal) there is no "working"—there is only noticing and becoming more aware. Sometimes, and often with practice, we might experience calmness and quieting as a by-product of practicing mindfulness—but that is not the necessary goal. There are many times when we are being mindful when we simply notice the chaos, incessant chatter, and inner critical voice of our mind. The act of noticing and continuing to work on letting go of judgment and remaining aware is the practice. We practice mindfulness to become more aware of the nature of our minds, more present, and more awake in our lives.

One colleague explained mindfulness using the following example, which I often share with my patients. Imagine there are boats traveling down a river, one after the other. The boats represent our thoughts, emotions, and sensations at any given point in time. Often, it is as if each passing boat drags us along in the water, pulling us away as if in tow. If I have the thought, "I'm so stupid," or an intense feeling of anxiety in my chest, those can pull me away and spiral me into increasingly negative thoughts or feelings of overwhelm. However, when we practice mindfulness, it is as if we are standing on the bank of the river watching the boats pass by one by one. From the safety of the bank, we can observe our emotions and thoughts as they arise and pass but we no longer get swept away by them. We still feel and experience these things. We can see our judgmental thoughts and our worries, and we can feel our anger or fear arising, but we don't get completely lost in it. In that little bit of space we've created by standing on the riverbank, we've given ourselves the power to observe and relate differently to our experience and choose our reactions.

This kind of attention can help us wake up to our lives in many new ways. When we learn to bring this quality of mindful attention into our day, it can provide a kind of antidote to some of the challenges I discussed in the previous chapter. It offers an antidote to being caught in the chronic activation of the fight-or-flight response, because we begin to see that the stress response that we experience is based on a *perception* of threat, not necessarily an actual threat.

Once I recognize that I am being triggered by a false alarm, I no longer *have to* react to that alarm as if it is a life-threatening emergency. If I know the smoke alarm is going off due to toast burning in my toaster, I don't have to pull out the fire extinguisher or call the fire department. When I can remind myself that there is no bear chasing me—thus calming the neural circuitry in my brain—this helps me to see the bigger picture and access greater resources. There is also space to be with my discomfort or anxiety about a situation with greater compassion.

Additionally, mindfulness can help us to identify our "false alarms" as helpful signals that *something* needs our attention—even if that might simply involve attending to our own internal emotions and thoughts. If my smoke alarm is going off because the toast is burning, I am not going to ignore it. It signals me to take appropriate action. I might open the windows, unplug my toaster, and clean out the debris. Developing a healthy mindset around stress can be essential to mitigate its impact. Remember, our stress response in and of itself is not a bad thing—it is healthy and adaptive in certain situations. When we pay attention, we can use short-term stress to motivate, mobilize, and energize us to perform optimally. We can also use the signals from our stress response to recognize when we need to replenish and reset so that we don't stay in a state of chronic activation. Mindfulness helps us attend to whatever is arising. The goal here is not to get rid of stress or be stress free (an impossible goal) but to be *stress smart*. The flashlight of mindful awareness helps us to see what is there, so we can respond more thoughtfully.

This kind of mindful attention can also be an antidote to our tendency to operate on automatic pilot and go through the motions of our day unconsciously. When we carry our flashlight around with us in our front pocket, and remember to pull it out throughout the day, we are no longer helpless to our automatic reactions; instead, we can choose more skillfully how we want to respond. Sometimes, that choice might be as simple as remembering to send some compassion to ourselves for whatever we are experiencing. Sometimes it might be choosing to enjoy the gifts of the present moment. Mindfulness can also help us see how our narratives and the stories in our head are adding to our unhappiness. When we notice this, we invite in the possibility to construct more helpful narratives that can empower our lives. In addition, mindfulness can offer us a way to be with our emotional discomfort by recognizing and naming what is there and accepting it with kindness, rather than ignoring or avoiding it to our own detriment. (We will explore some of these latter benefits of mindfulness in subsequent chapters).

So one way we can use the flashlight is informally, as we go through our day. The more we remember to carry it with us *and* pull it out and turn it on (to pay attention with non-judgment, kindness, and intentionality), the more we can choose how we want to respond to our stressors and engage in life to the fullest. I will share some illustrations of this shortly.

We can use the flashlight in two distinct ways: by pointing it at the outer world and pointing it at our inner world. Both are important.

When we shine the flashlight on our inner world, we are noticing our own body sensations, thoughts and emotions from the banks of the river. We are taking inventory of our own inner landscape. When we engage our attention in this way, we naturally invite in an integration of our mind and body, because our thoughts, emotions and sensations each have physical and mental aspects. For example, when we notice we are feeling hurt, we may also connect in with a sensation of heaviness around our heart; when we notice that we are ruminating about a future worry, we also may notice the contraction of our muscles that accompanies those worry thoughts. When we feel pain in our bodies, we also might notice that our mind immediately wants to attach a story to it (for example, "oh no, what if something is wrong!").

When we point a flashlight at our outer world, we notice what is happening in front of us in this moment. We snap ourselves out of our automatic pilot trance and come back to our senses, literally. With our flashlight pointing outward, we might see the sunlight falling through the window, or the smile of the stranger on the street. We might hear the buzz of our toothbrush or the tone of concern in a friend's voice. We might taste the sweetness of an apple and create the opening in which to savor what is there. We might feel the sensation of our feet as they make contact with the ground beneath us. When we become present in this way, we wake up to the richness that life has to offer us that we might otherwise easily miss. When we point our flashlight to the outer world and intentionally pay attention to what is in front of us, we connect our mind and body by experiencing the world more fully through our senses. We *embody* the moment.

As I said previously, we can use our flashlight informally by simply remembering to carry it with us throughout our day. However, it isn't quite as easy as it sounds. Remember, there are many ways in which our brain naturally pulls us away from the present moment. For many of us, it is as if we walk around with a flashlight that has a weak battery that flickers on and off frequently (more off than on). Thus, practice and repetition become very important for us to make changes in our brain and in our lives. So in addition to informal practice, if we want to strengthen our flashlight so that it can shine brightly and more consistently throughout our day, it can help to engage in formal practice.

Formal practice, or mindfulness meditation, is one way of strengthening this flashlight. When we set aside formal time in which to focus our attention mindfully on something in our internal or external world (it could be focusing our attention on our breathing, our internal mental states, such as our thoughts and emotions as they arise and pass, or on something in our external world such as the feel of the ground beneath our feet) we strengthen the neural circuits in our brain that focus our attention and bring us into this moment. There are many benefits of practicing mindfulness, including: increased immune functioning; greater internal stability and clarity; improvements in attention and focus; greater mental health, especially in the areas of depression, anxiety, and addictions; increased empathy; greater resilience to face challenges; and an improved sense of well-being (Siegel, 2010).

Let's explore some of the ways that you can use your flashlight to improve your well-being. Some of these examples involve using mindfulness more informally, and some offer suggestions for short formal practice.

How Mindfulness (the Flashlight) Can Help Us Calm the False Alarm

When we become mindfully aware of our stress response rising and our false alarm sounding as we go through our day, we can begin to respond more skillfully to the challenges that we face in our lives, rather than reacting from a primitive, automatic place. In this way, we can actually learn to use our stress to work for us, not against us. When we observe stress rising, we can use it as a signal to pause and notice what is needed. Here are some examples:

Jake was driving to work on his long commute, as he typically does, having left himself just enough time to get to work with the usual amount of traffic. He hadn't anticipated the detour that sent him completely out of the way, adding additional time to his travels. As the minutes passed with traffic stalled, he found himself becoming increasingly stressed and anxious, in a situation about which he could do nothing. His typical and automatic response to these kinds of situations was to rant and rave, completely unleashing his frustration, anger and helplessness in a kind of fight-or-flight response tirade. However, he had recently begun practicing the flashlight strategy, and in this particular moment remembered to use it. Instead of automatically being swept away by his anger and frustration, he began to notice it. He observed the tension building in his body, and he noticed his heart rate increasing. He recognized the usual pattern of response that he saw himself descending into. He tried to picture himself sitting on the bank of the river, watching his stress thoughts pass by ("What an idiot! I should have left myself enough time. I'll never make it to work at this rate.") These thoughts kept coming, but as he watched them, they seemed to have a little less hold on him. Jake recognized that his fight-or-flight response was kicking into full force, but he was able to name what was happening. He looked around himself. There were no lions chasing him. He smiled. Yes, this was a false alarm. In fact, what he noticed was some of the other drivers, who were clearly frustrated, too, and also had places to be. He felt some empathy for them and realized he wasn't alone in his frustration. Jake pictured a meter going from one to ten, in which one represented a minor glitch in his day, and ten represented a true emergency. He realized this situation was about a three on the scale, even though it felt like an eight. He reminded himself that he was safe in this moment, albeit frustrated. He also was able to recognize that as undesirable as it might be to arrive late to work, this was not the end of the world and he could talk with his boss about staying a bit later to make up for the time.

Aisha had worked a double shift and was coming home from a long and tiring day. She had spent a lot of time during her work breaks on the phone with rehabilitation facilities, trying to arrange for her mother to be moved from the hospital, where she recently had hip surgery, to a rehab center. This was the second time in a year that her mother had been in the hospital, and she was worried about her long-term prognosis. Her two teenage children were still awake when she arrived home, and she was happy to see them. This happiness quickly melted away, however, when she saw the dishes piled in the sink, the dog with no food, the laundry still unfolded, and the kids glued to their video games. To make matters worse, her husband seemed oblivious to all of this, as he was engrossed in a TV show. Aisha could feel herself going from zero to sixty. Typically, she would explode in anger at her family members, in what felt like a justified reaction (her kids for not doing their chores, and her husband for not helping and making sure the kids did what was asked of them).

Practicing her flashlight strategy did not feel easy in this moment, but she recognized that as soon as she walked in the door, she had an immediate feeling of threat, as if she were being metaphorically attacked due to her unmet needs. She felt an equally strong desire to fight back and attack. She also knew this response never ended well. Instead of going in for the usual attack, she was able to linger in the doorway a few moments. She had practiced mindful breathing (following her breath in and out, bringing her attention to each inhalation and exhalation, over and over) and she decided this was as good a time as any to do it. When she practiced it previously, it had been during times when she was not being triggered. This was very different. She could feel herself shaking with anger, could see her mind racing, but she kept trying to bring her attention to her breathing as she acknowledged her hurt and angry feelings. She let herself feel the hurt and anger, without reacting to it in her usual explosive way. She looked around and saw the messy house, and her children and husband oblivious, but safe and healthy. There was no fire, no life-threatening emergency, but there was a situation that needed to be dealt with. Taking those few moments helped Aisha step out of attack mode, even though she was still upset. In the space of a few moments, she was able to think about how she wanted to handle the situation, which included telling her husband how upset she was, and then sitting down with the children and establishing clear expectations and consequences, and having them complete their chores before bed that night.

Serika was headed to a party on campus, when she started to experience a panic attack. She broke out in a sweat, her heart began to race, her face became flushed, and she started to feel slightly nauseous. In the past, these symptoms would have freaked her out and spiraled her into a full blown panic that would have stopped her in her tracks and sent her to her room for the night. She would have been extremely scared by what she was experiencing. But this time, Serika understood what was happening in her body. This was a false alarm and a healthy, adaptive response to a perceived physical threat (even though rationally, she knew there was no actual threat). She was able to observe her body preparing to fight or flee with more curiosity than fear, and recognized it would pass. She noticed how uncomfortable it was for her, but she also knew that she could ride it out and she didn't have to fight it. She reminded herself that she was safe and that it's all right to feel anxious about new social situations. She felt compassion for her scared self, and was able to acknowledge this, in contrast to the past when she would berate herself for feeling anxious. She focused her attention on the sensation and sound of her feet making contact with the ground with each step she took. This helped her to feel grounded and anchored even as the intensity of her emotions washed over her. Whenever she noticed her mind pulling her away (for example, thinking "Oh God, not another panic attack! When will these stop? I can't stand this."), she brought her attention and focus back into the sensations of walking and told herself she was safe in the moment. By not reacting to the panic symptoms as a true emergency and by learning ways to help her body feel safe, she was able to ride out the passing storm and continue with her evening plans.

How Mindfulness (the Flashlight) Can Help Us Throw the Switch on Our Default Mode Network & Wake Up to Our Lives (Becoming Present to What is Here)

Remember that stuck dial that keeps us in a mind-wandering mode much of the time? Well, it turns out there is another "dial," or series of brain networks called the task-positive network, which is activated when we perform attention-demanding tasks. It is also active when we consciously direct our attention to our internal body sensations and when we use our five senses to engage in the world around us. It comes "on line" when we are engaged in various forms of mindfulness, and it acts as a kind of switch that dials down the activity in the default mode network (McKinnon, 2014). The good news is that we can learn to activate it more often every time we use our flashlight.

As Derick began to practice carrying a flashlight around with him, he realized how much of the day he was lost in mind-wandering. He hadn't recognized it before, but now he could see the frequent tendency of his mind to pull him away from the present moment into thoughts about future events (thinking about what is coming next and getting through the day, rather than being in it.) This took up more of his day than he had realized, and showed up even in surprising ways. For example, he hadn't realized how often his mind was focused somewhere else when his children were talking to him. He didn't realize how often he was thinking about the next meal while still eating his current one.

After he had practiced carrying around his flashlight and still found himself frequently lost in mind-wandering, his first inclination was to criticize himself for not being more present, and for not being able to "get it right" and stay more focused on what was in front of him. However, with some guidance, he recognized that this was just his mind going into self-judgment, which in turn perpetuated his ruminations. He also was relieved to learn that this was normal and happened even to seasoned practitioners of mindfulness. There was no perfection to strive for; it was only about letting go of judgment and bringing himself back again and again when he noticed his mind pulling him away. This might happen three times in a day, or it might be one hundred. Freeing himself from unrealistic expectations (of "needing" to be present most of the time), he began to relax and appreciate the small moments when he did catch himself and turn back into *this* moment. When he caught his mind wandering while talking with his children, he refocused his attention on their expressions and the emotional tone behind their words. When he did this, he felt more connected. When he found himself planning the next meal while eating the current one, he refocused his attention on eating slowly and experiencing the tastes and textures of his food. Little moments in his day became richer as he gradually found it easier to bring himself back to what was happening right here and now.

Maria, as you may recall from Chapter One, was frequently pulled into negative ruminations that could spiral her into depressive thinking. Once she started paying attention and carrying her flashlight with her, she was able to catch herself when she started getting pulled into these unhelpful thought loops. She found that once she became aware that she was caught up in mind-wandering, the most helpful way to step out of it was to bring her attention to whatever she could experience in the present moment through her five senses.

Here is a quick sample of her day with and without the flashlight.

Maria's day *without* the flashlight:

Maria wakes up and her mind starts racing forward into the day about how stressful it is going to be with three big meetings scheduled and then an evening meeting with her accountant. As she is in the shower, she starts thinking about how she should have made different financial decisions five years ago. She begins playing out in her mind all of the things that might have been different if she had made better choices back then.

Now in a bad mood without being aware why, she snaps at her spouse as she rushes to eat her breakfast. While eating, her mind wanders to a comment her spouse made last week that she found irritating, and unbeknownst to her, she becomes increasingly tense and disconnected.

On the way to work, her mind wanders to some of the stressors that she had to deal with last week that have since been resolved, but nonetheless add to her current experience of stress.

Maria's day *with* the flashlight:

Maria wakes up and her mind starts to wander to the meetings ahead. She catches herself and refocuses her flashlight by taking a moment to look out her window and notice the sun falling across the lawn, casting shadows; the squirrels chasing one another on the wet grass; and the red robin which just took off skyward from the tree branch.

In the shower when she notices her mind wandering, she makes a point of smelling the aroma of the shampoo and soap, and letting the feel of the warm water soothe her. She is still aware of wandering thoughts, but they have less hold on her. She catches herself being a bit irritable with her spouse, but then apologizes and gives her a warm embrace before she leaves.

While eating breakfast her mind wanders off, but she catches herself long enough to enjoy a few good sips of the strong coffee she made.

On the train to work, she made a point of playing her favorite music, and she found this energizing and uplifting. Listening to music on the train to work was a regular time in her day when she had decided to practice being more mindful.

How Mindfulness Can Help Us Hit the Pause Button and Reset

Practicing mindfulness formally, even in short increments, can have a beneficial impact on our day. I am a big fan of using a three-minute mindful pause during the day, both as an opportunity to take inventory (at any time,) and as a chance to hit the pause button when I sense stress rising. (You'll find an example of how to do a three-minute mindful pause at the end of this chapter).

As one personal example of this, I remember a particular evening years ago when my then-teenage son hadn't done some chores that I had requested. I found myself feeling increasingly stressed, frustrated and angry. In fact, I felt that I was ready to snap at him. I recognized the "flashlight" could come in handy, so I set the timer app on my phone (a mindful bell) for three minutes. At times I might unknowingly ignore these body signals, but remembering to use my flashlight helped me to take a beneficial pause. (While I don't always remember to use the tools I have, the more I practice the easier it is to access them as I go through my daily life.) As I turned my flashlight inward, I became aware of emotions that felt disproportionate to the situation at hand. Holding the flashlight there further, I became aware of some surprising sadness underneath the anger. Taking a curious look, I recognized that this sadness had to do with my teenage son growing up and pulling away from me. Once I recognized this, something in me relaxed, as my feelings felt acknowledged. This pause gave me the space to respond from a more aware place, addressing the undone chores while not spilling over some of these other emotions into my interactions with my son.

Morgan had been practicing short mindfulness exercises at home. Lately, an employee, who hasn't been working up to the company's expectations, has been triggering her at work. Typically, her reaction had been to blurt out whatever was on her mind to the employee, often saying things in an angry tone that didn't match who she wanted to be as a boss. After practicing some mindfulness at home, she decided she would take a three-minute mindful pause at work before approaching the employee. Doing this allowed her to recognize her own anxiety about having everything run smoothly, and the alarm this triggered in her when things did not. As she became aware of these feelings, they reminded her of earlier times in her life when things felt chaotic and unpredictable, when she was at the whim of a partner who was unstable and made unhealthy choices. Bringing some awareness to this alarm response she was experiencing allowed her to gain more perspective on the current situation and approach the employee with more patience and openness, from a less threatened place. Morgan found that taking a few minutes for a mindful pause in her day helped her to be the compassionate boss that she wanted to be. She also discovered that responding this way had a positive effect on her employees, who were much more responsive and motivated to make changes.

Jovana began to notice how high strung and depleted she felt much of the day; a feeling that had become so familiar to her that she considered it normal. Every day, she had to balance her part-time job as a nurse with her role as a mom of a special needs son who required 24/7 attention, a younger son, and her aging mother who lived with them. She found that she spent most of her time caretaking and had very little time for herself. The idea of meditating had always seemed like something for other people with the luxury of time, but it didn't seem accessible to her. When Jovana learned about the three-minute mindful pause, she decided this might be something she could fit into her day. She made a point of setting aside three minutes for herself at the beginning, middle and end of her day, including right before her older son came home from school. She had been so focused on taking care of everyone else's needs that she hadn't realized she never spent time attending to her own. Taking even just these three minutes to take inventory of how she was feeling and what she was experiencing was deeply replenishing for her. Sometimes, she was able to feel glimmers of a deep, inner calmness and a permission to relax within these moments. At other times, she just noticed her feelings of overwhelm from a little bit of a distance. At these latter times, she would put her hand on her heart and send herself some compassion, acknowledging all that she does, and sending some breath to the tight places in her body. Taking these small moments in her day helped her to experience more ease and energy, and to have more moments when she could be present with her sons.

Our flashlight is our steadiest companion, and as we strengthen its light and remember to use it more consistently throughout the day, it can help us in a myriad of ways. As noted earlier in this chapter, one of the gifts of carrying mindful awareness with us is that it can help us to notice when our fight-or-flight response is turned on, and when we are experiencing a false alarm. When we learn to come back to THIS moment, we interrupt the false alarm and invite in the recognition that in this moment we are OK. This helps to create a felt sense of safety within. Often, the threats that our minds drum up reside in the past, live in our imagined future, or aren't as bad as we perceive them to be. Interrupting the false alarm with our own mindful observation helps to turn down that primitive part of our brain, and allows us access to the higher thinking part of our brain that can see a bigger picture, hold things in perspective, and choose wise action from the inner resources available to us. This can be immensely helpful to cope with whatever challenges and stressors we are facing in our day.

Taking even a few minutes for mindful breathing can help to dial down the part of our autonomic nervous system responsible for the stress response (the sympathetic nervous system) and can help turn on the "relaxation response"—controlled by a part of our autonomic nervous system called the parasympathetic nervous system. I have seen this first hand in my office when I use biofeedback with patients (a computer program that can show what is happening inside the body).

An important point I want to emphasize is that mindfulness is about observing whatever is arising without judgment, whether it is pleasant, unpleasant or neutral. It is not about *trying* to relax. However, holding a space for the whole of our experience, being compassionate with ourselves, and noticing our inner sensations, thoughts, emotions and our own breath can often have a beneficial side effect of bringing more balance and synchrony between the two branches of our autonomic nervous system, and creating a felt sense of greater harmony and balance within.

Our flashlight can also help us step out of automatic pilot and our default mode of going through the motions of our day, lost in our heads. When we step out of automatic pilot, we create choice and begin to see options that we might not have seen before. We also come back into our senses and open up to the experiences that are in front of us, allowing us to become more present and alive.

An Anchor in the Storm

Before ending this chapter, I would like to share a story about how the formal practicing of mindfulness helped me through a significant personal challenge. I share this in part to illustrate how formal practice during periods when we are not under the influence of the "false alarm" can help us later during more stressful times. When we practice some form of mindfulness (returning our wandering attention over and over to an external or internal object of focus, without judging our experience as right or wrong, good or bad), we help to establish a kind of inner anchor of stability to which we can return. Imagine a ship that has dropped its anchor. The waters may be calm and peaceful, or stormy and turbulent, but deep underneath the surface the anchor holds the ship securely so there is a felt sense of safety amidst the passing storms. This felt sense of security—our inner anchor—can become a familiar place to return to as we practice formal meditation. We need not quiet our minds or achieve perfect calm or bliss to experience the benefits. Sometimes the practice is simply noticing the passing waves and storms, and holding on securely to the ship's anchor (for example, our own breath).

This kind of formal practice might take the form of sitting and following our breath in and out—all the while noticing the crazy places our mind wants to take us—or the wild emotions rocking around inside of us—and gently bringing our attention back again and again to our breath coming in and out. It might take the form of movement-based meditation, such as yoga—in which we practice bringing our attention over and over again to the sensation of our bodies moving through space, even as we notice the self-judgments and wanderings of our mind. It could involve walking meditation, bringing your focus to the feel of your feet making contact with the ground, or keeping your focus on an object in nature while walking. For some people, prayer can be a form of meditation. There is no one, right way. Experiment with what works for you and practice for just a few minutes if you like. Practicing for a few minutes a day is more beneficial than setting yourself up with a big plan you can't maintain and eventually abandon. Choose something small that you can practice consistently and let that be your starting point.

One of my favorite forms of moving meditation is swimming, and I did this frequently during my first pregnancy. I chose certain mantras that I would repeat to myself as I swam back and forth, and sometimes I just focused on the rhythm of my breathing. I did this in part because it helped me to feel that inner anchor of stability within. This was helpful for me given my type A and anxious nature, and the many worries I experienced during that pregnancy. I found it calming. And I also did this in part as a kind of preparation for childbirth, since I planned on having a natural delivery.

As much as I prepared myself for many scenarios of what childbirth might be like, I couldn't possibly have prepared myself for what was to unfold. Eight weeks before I was due to give birth, my husband went to Florida for a business trip. I ended up in the emergency room with what seemed like premature contractions that weekend, and was sent home. Not more than a few hours after my husband returned home (on the earliest flight he could get), I started having more contractions and ended up back in the hospital. This time, I was sent home with orders for complete bed rest for the rest of my pregnancy. However, in the wee hours of the night, I began having severe abdominal pain. I have a pretty high threshold for pain, but this eventually became unbearable. Thinking it was the stomach flu, I held off waking my husband as long as possible to let him sleep. When I did wake him around 6:30 am, the pain and nausea I was experiencing was overwhelming. My memory of the ride back to the hospital is mostly a blur, except for remembering it took what seemed like an interminable amount of time to get there due to the bumper to bumper rush hour traffic. I still was convinced I had the stomach flu. Once I was situated at the hospital and in good care, I told my husband to go to work for a few hours, as I thought there was nothing he could do for me at that moment.

Little did I know that several hours and many tests later, I would be having an emergency delivery. I had actually been feeling much better. My stomach pain and nausea had dissipated. So I was pretty shocked when my doctor came in and told me that I had preeclampsia with something called HELLP syndrome (which was affecting my liver functions and putting my life in danger). So the baby needed to be delivered immediately, almost eight weeks early, and my doctor informed me she was going to break my water before I could even call my husband. The hope was that with an injection of the drug Pitocin I would have a quick delivery.

Somewhere around this time, I started meditating by following my breath. I had done it many times before and I knew how to find that familiar anchor of breath and keep coming back to it. I can't tell you exactly why or how I didn't freak out with everything that was unfolding.

For someone who is a natural worrier, I can't explain why I didn't go into a complete panic mode about whether I would be OK (as my liver function kept declining) and whether my baby would be OK (coming into the world almost 2 months early). There are plenty of times, even now in life, when little things still throw me, much less the bigger things. But I was able to grab onto my breath like a lifeline and stay focused on it. My breath steadied me through the news that I was not progressing fast enough with the delivery to keep me out of danger, and I would need an emergency C-section. It steadied me through the ten minutes when they raced me from one room to the next, with a team of six doctors by my side prepping me for the C-section. And it steadied me through the news that they would medicate me heavily immediately after the birth to put me into a twenty-four hour deep sleep to prevent me from having post-birth seizures. Somehow through it all, I kept coming back to my breath, and to those mantras and affirmations that I had practiced while swimming in the pool, and I felt an inner calmness that helped me through the experience. I am convinced that having practiced mindfulness meditation helped me get through that life-threatening emergency in a way that I would not have been able to do otherwise. (P.S. I gave birth to a healthy baby girl, 3 pounds, 6 ounces and I recovered fully).

Below are three short practices that you can try out and use within the course of your day:

Practice One: Turning Down the False Alarm

1. Make note of some of the signals and warning signs you experience when stress begins to rise (e.g., tense muscles, clenching jaw, increased irritability, shallow breathing, snapping at others, panicked thoughts).

2. Bring your flashlight into your day and notice when you start to experience any warning signs. Notice when your false alarm is starting to sound (or catch it even before it sounds if possible).

You might practice this now by calling up a typical trigger for you. When you notice stress present, see it as a helpful signal for you to pause and attend to what is there.

3.   Once you become aware of a stress response occurring, take a few minutes to use this Stress Acronym to help you. Think of the word "STRESS" as soon as you become aware of your stress response and spell out the word using the acronym below. Read it through and then see below for further instructions.

> **S**top. Stand (or sit) in stillness; feel stability in my body.
>
> **T**ake time to breathe.
>
> **R**ecognize my thoughts.
>
> **E**mbrace my emotions.
>
> **S**end myself support and compassion.
>
> **S**ee what is needed.

Stop. Stand (or sit) in stillness, feel stability in my body. Focus on the sensation of your feet on the ground. Imagine that you are a strong tree deeply rooted or an immovable mountain withstanding a passing storm. Remind yourself that you are safe in this moment, despite the difficulty of what you are experiencing.

Take time to breathe. Try this quick breathing exercise that can be done in a minute using what I call "elevator" breathing. Allow the focus of your attention to travel downward in your body, as if stopping at floors on an elevator. First, notice the breath at your nose and face, feeling the breath flowing in and our through your nostrils. Next, notice the breath flowing in and out through the center of your chest or your "heart center," becoming aware of sensations there. Finally, bring your focus down to your belly and note the rise and fall of your belly with each breath cycle. As you do this, try putting one hand on your heart, and one hand on your belly, with gentle pressure. This can often have a calming and soothing effect on your nervous system (Siegel, 2015).

Recognize my thoughts. Name whatever you are thinking by saying "I notice that..." For example, if you are stuck in traffic you might say: "I notice that I am having catastrophic thoughts about being late for work and ruining my whole day." See if you can allow these thoughts to be there, without judging them as good or bad. Try instead to take a curious look at whatever is there and notice how it is contributing to your stress. (We will work more with our thinking using the tool of "the diet" in the next chapter).

Embrace my emotions: Allow yourself to feel whatever is there and name your feelings. Is it sadness, fear, jealousy, anger, hurt or something else? As in the previous step, see if you might add the words "I notice that..." (for example, I notice that I am feeling angry) without judging your feelings as good or bad. Try to be willing to acknowledge whatever you are feeling. We tend to push our uncomfortable feelings away, but interestingly, when we turn toward them they tend to soften and ease. (We will work more with our emotions using the tool of "the door" in a subsequent chapter).

Send myself support and compassion. Extend kindness and care to yourself, the way you would a good friend. Acknowledge that whatever you are going through is difficult, but know that you will get through it.

See what is needed. From the farthest vantage point, look at the situation at hand, see the big picture in perspective and choose the actions that would be most helpful. When we take this kind of mindful pause and work to calm our nervous system, we can then access the higher, thinking part of our brain, our prefrontal cortex, to help us respond more skillfully.

Practice Two: Coming into Our Senses

Pick a time of day when you tend to do something routinely. Some examples might include brushing your teeth, taking a shower, eating breakfast, driving to work, walking across the street during your lunch break to get food, or something else that is a regular part of your day. Make the decision that every time you engage in this activity you will use it as an opportunity to practice mindfulness. Starting with just a few minutes the first time, make an intentional effort to pay attention to whatever you experience through your five senses. For example, if you choose walking across the street at noon to buy your lunch you might notice the feeling of the air against your skin, the warmth of the sun on your face, the noises of the people around you, the aromas in the air, etc. You might purposely walk a bit more slowly to take in the whole experience.

Pairing this kind of mindfulness practice with something you already do routinely can make it easier to do it consistently. Having a few minutes of consistent practice like this can make it easier to notice other times in the day when you are caught in mental loops, false alarms and other mental activities that take you away from the here and now of this moment.

Practice Three: A Three Minute Mindful Pause

This practice can be done at any time. It can be helpful to use it when you feel your stress level beginning to rise, but it may also be helpful at the beginning or end of the day as a way to take inventory of your internal landscape and notice what is there. You might consider doing this before you have a challenging conversation. It can also be a helpful way to step out of the busyness of the day and replenish yourself or hit the "reset" button.

To get started, set a timer with a mindful bell or soothing chime for three minutes. (There are many apps available to download on your phone that offer this.) Use the sound of the bell to allow your body to settle in where you are seated. Take a moment to inhabit your body. In our running around, we often become disconnected from our bodies. Take a moment to feel your feet on the ground, notice the sensations in the souls of your feet, and the support of the chair beneath you. Notice your breath flowing in and out. Feel the sensation of your breath with each inhalation and each exhalation. No need to change anything, just notice. Allow your breath to help you come into this moment. Notice any ways that stress may be showing up in your body. See if you can let go of things from earlier in the day or week. Putting aside your to-do list, see if you can arrive right here, right now. Give your body the invitation to let go of whatever you don't need to be holding in this moment.

Your mind will likely fill with thoughts. That's OK. That's normal. Notice if those thoughts contribute to your stress in any way. Gently guide your attention back to your breath and body. Sense the stillness of your body, even if your mind is quite active. Give yourself these few minutes to settle in right where you are, to meet yourself wherever you are. Notice whatever emotions are present and see if you might give them space. Whatever you are feeling, just notice it. Take inventory of where you are right now. At the end of the three minutes, gently bring your awareness back into the room.

~ Go back to the questions at the end of the introduction, where you wrote down some of the challenges you currently face. Pick one or more of these and think about how you might use the flashlight to help you when this challenge arises. Write how using the flashlight informally, as you go through the course of your day, might allow you greater choice to respond skillfully and wisely to the challenges at hand.

~ Write out how you might practice using the flashlight more formally, such as in the three-minute mindful pause, to help you face some of your current challenges.

Suggestion for Further Practice

Experiment with setting up a short, daily mindfulness practice. Pick a length of time that you know you can stick with, whether it might be a three minute mindful pause or five-minute or perhaps ten-minute practice. (Some of my patients set a reminder bell on their phone to go off periodically throughout the day to remind them to pause for a moment and be mindful.) Choose a brief period of time to start.

There are many free downloadable apps available that offer mindfulness timers and guided meditations of varying lengths. The more you practice consistently, even for short periods of time, the more the flashlight will become an accessible resource for you to use in your life.

CHAPTER THREE

The Diet: Nourishing Ourselves Through Our Thoughts and Self-Compassion

I HAD AN INTERESTING EXPERIENCE on a train ride returning from New York City to Boston. I hadn't slept well the night before and was cranky and irritable. (I'm someone who is quite affected by lack of sleep.) I found myself caught up in my thoughts, worrying about how I was going to have the energy and attentiveness to see an afternoon and evening's worth of patients. I had hoped to rest a bit on the train, but so far, I hadn't been able to fall asleep. I was disappointed that the train was so crowded that I couldn't get a seat next to a window which I could lean up against. Then, onto the train came a mother and her adolescent daughter, who took the seats right across from me. It became apparent very quickly that this teen was unhappy, and she began to complain and argue loudly with her mother. It was not the quiet train ride I had hoped for!

My mind filled with thoughts of getting up and moving, trying to find the "quiet" car, putting on my headphones to block out the unwanted noise. My mind started to spin further into thoughts of not being a good therapist later in the day because I would be so tired that I wouldn't be fully present, and then I started worrying about how I was going to sleep that night, and what if I didn't sleep well again. My thoughts were quickly spiraling.

When I overheard this mother-daughter pair arguing about the teen forgetting her headphones, it occurred to me that I could offer her mine. As I listened for a pause in the heated conversation to offer the headphones, I took a closer look at the mother sitting across from me. It struck me that it wasn't too long ago that I was walking in this woman's shoes. There were so many times that I could recall when my own children were having meltdowns in public places. And I remembered the helplessness and embarrassment I felt at those times. That moment of empathy snapped me awake and out of my negative, spiraling thoughts, as I felt compassion for this mother, and her daughter as well, who was clearly struggling. My thoughts shifted away from my own catastrophic and negative thinking to thoughts of connection for the humanness within us all. I was able to send myself some compassion, too, because I recognized the younger part of myself that could easily become anxious when circumstances were out of my control. The shift in my thinking was like at first looking through glasses with a pinhole opening, and then suddenly being able to see 360 degrees around me. I felt an openness and spaciousness that hadn't been there before. This was such a tiny moment in my day, and yet my mood and energy completely transformed so that I could show up more aligned with whom I wanted to be that day.

Tool Two: The Diet

When we pay attention to where our mind goes—to the narratives that we attach to our experiences and the language through which we interpret the world (the noisy person in the movie theater)—we start to see the diet of thoughts that we feed to ourselves all day long. Sometimes this diet is nourishing, but for many of us, this diet often lacks nutrients. Sometimes it is downright unhealthy.

Let's take a closer look at some of the ways our language traps us, how our narratives contribute to our suffering, and how we can learn to feed ourselves a healthier diet of thoughts.

Noticing Our Diet of Thoughts

When we pay attention to what we are eating in a traditional diet, we can learn to make more nourishing choices. The first step, then, involves noticing what we are eating. The second step is choosing to nourish ourselves with healthy foods. We can do this with the diet of thoughts that we feed ourselves as well.

The flashlight can help us with the first step. Besides helping us notice when we are triggered by false alarms or stuck in mind-wandering, the flashlight can help us notice when the noisy person in the movie theater is in action. In a dark theater, it might be hard to see where this voice comes from, but shine the light of awareness on it and suddenly we have some options that weren't previously available to us. We can see the voice for what it is and not take it too seriously (Oh, it's just that noisy person at the movie theater again—oh well), or we can tell ourselves a different story that may be more helpful. The flashlight allows us to recognize the impact of the language that we use and the narratives we attach to our experiences. It can be especially helpful in identifying the running commentary and inner dialog of our minds that is often critical, negative, extreme, distorted and unhelpful. With this awareness, we can choose a diet that is more accurate, helpful, nourishing and empowering for us.

What is important to recognize is that the noisy person sitting next to us in the theater is perceiving the movie through a particular lens. Often that lens is quite limited, based on old patterns and old conditioning that no longer serve us. (We will explore this in greater detail in Chapter Seven). The noisy person in the movie theater can wear many disguises. The more we can recognize these disguises, the more we can do something about it. I will reveal some of the disguises and suggest some diets that might be helpful for each one. There is no one diet that fits all. We may get pulled into different kinds of thought traps at different times and in each circumstance, a different diet may help the most to nourish us. Note, too, that when I am referring to "diet" here, I am really talking about a lifestyle choice, not a fad diet. It is something that we can work at each day, a work in progress, that has no particular endpoint. It is nourishing ourselves each day with healthy thoughts that adds up over time for our health and wellness.

The Diet of Realistic/Accurate Thinking Versus Distorted Thinking

Whether we like it or not, our minds tend toward catastrophic thinking. That noisy person at the movie theater often overestimates the likelihood of bad things happening, and also often exaggerates how bad a situation will be. This helped our ancestors survive true threats, but it can get in the way of our well-being in our modern lives. Think about how often we say these kinds of things to ourselves: "Oh God, this is going to be awful; That was such a disaster; That just ruined my day; I'll never be able to deal with that . . ." As you may have noticed, the noisy person in the movie theater can set off that false smoke alarm with this kind of language. In the book, *Words Can Change Your Brain,* the authors describe how even a single negative word can activate our amygdala, the fear center in the brain that turns on our fight-or-flight response (Newberg and Waldman, 2013).

Even when we don't actually believe that a situation is a "disaster," using this kind of language can have a negative impact on our mood and outlook. To do a quick experiment, say the alarm and disaster statements from the previous paragraph out loud and then pause and notice how your body feels. When I have asked even some of my child patients to do this, they immediately note that their body feels tense and tight; their chest feels heavy; and they feel a sense of hopelessness or even doom. Now take a moment and say the following to yourself: "This is difficult, but I'll find a way to cope; That was very disappointing; I'm upset that X happened in my day, but I got through it; As hard as this is for me, I have resources I can draw on to help me deal with this." Now pause and notice where those words land in your body. What feelings and sensations do they evoke in you? When I say these words to myself, I notice my body begins to relax and I feel more openness around the center of my chest. Even though we might not think that words affect our bodies, the mind-body connection can be more powerful than we realize.

As simple as it sounds, in order to step out of this distorted thought trap, we must first recognize we are in it. Then, we can work to tweak our language to make it more accurate, to feed ourselves a healthier diet. Notice in the previous examples that they didn't say, "This is going to be great," or "I just had an amazing day." There is nothing wrong with saying those things if you believe them, but the words we choose must be accurate and reflect our actual experience. It isn't about pretending everything is fine if we believe it isn't. Instead, we can perceive when our thinking is inaccurate, distorted, extreme, or untrue, and change it so that it more accurately reflects the reality of the situation. Sometimes, we may recognize that there is more than one way to view a situation, and that can allow us to choose a more helpful perspective.

Some questions we can ask ourselves to help support a healthy diet include:

- Is this really true, or am I thinking in extremes or absolutes?

- Do I have any evidence to support this statement, or do I have evidence to suggest that there may be other alternatives that are more accurate?

- Is there another way to look at this situation that I haven't considered?

- How might I change the language to more accurately reflect my inner strengths, and the resources available to me?

- Is there a more helpful, believable version of this story that would serve me better?

Consider the following: Bart had a presentation to give at work but he wasn't fully prepared. During the presentation, he realized people were tuning out and not listening attentively to what he said. They seemed bored and disinterested. Afterwards, he found himself feeling quite down in the dumps. When he paid attention to the things he was telling himself about the situation, it sounded like the following: "That was a complete disaster! How am I ever going to get through another presentation? Everyone must be thinking about how incompetent I am. How am I ever going to show my face in the office?" No wonder he was feeling down! If you or I said those things to ourselves, we probably would feel the same way.

Once Bart recognized the thoughts that he was feeding himself, he was able to work on rewriting them for greater accuracy. Taking pen to paper, and writing out his old, negative thoughts and his revised, more accurate ones was helpful. Here is what he came up with: "I'm really disappointed that this presentation didn't go as well as it could have. I didn't spend adequate time preparing for it. People likely tuned out because it wasn't well organized and was hard to follow. I'm not the first person to give an imperfect presentation. There are plenty of ways that I have demonstrated my competence to my coworkers over the years. I'm embarrassed that it wasn't my best job, but there will be other opportunities to do better. In fact, it's a good lesson for next time to spend more time making sure my presentation is better organized and more engaging."

This new narrative was accurate and believable, and it was also more empowering for Bart. It allowed him to acknowledge and accept his imperfections, focus on his strengths and recognize his ability to succeed next time.

The Diet of "I notice this thought" Versus "I am this thought."

As discussed in Chapter Two, our thoughts can be like powerful ships traveling downstream, dragging us in their wake. It is easy to be swept away by our own negative thinking, and to accept our thoughts as reality or truth. When we experience our thoughts as fixed beliefs, and our narratives as reality, rather than as passing mental constructs, we can experience negative mood, rigidity of behavior and increased suffering. Life is challenging enough. Upsetting things happen sometimes. But attaching absolute statements to our difficult situations only adds insult to injury.

Sometimes we might even be aware that what we are saying to ourselves is not true, and yet we cannot disentangle ourselves from these powerful distorted thoughts. They may be ideas we have been telling ourselves for a very long time, perhaps as far back as childhood. Sometimes trying to change the language of these thoughts (like Bart did above) can feel too difficult in the moment. When this happens, it can help to simply notice the presence of the distorted thoughts and then let them pass down that river as we stand on the bank and watch. Just the act of noticing our thoughts creates some space and distance that can unhook us from our stories. We don't have to stop the thoughts (which, by the way, is nearly impossible to do and often makes them come all the more), or even change them in order to work with them. But we do have to notice that we are having the thoughts in the first place, from a mindful, observing place, to detach from their hold. As Tara Brach teaches, we can remind ourselves that our thoughts are "real but not true." When we can hold our experience in a compassionate presence, this helps us to disconnect from the "trance of unworthiness" that so often grips us (Brach, 2013).

Consider Serika, who discovers she is feeding herself the following diet:

- I'm so anxious.

- I'm such a loser (that I can't go to this party).

- I'm too anxious to raise my hand in class.

As you can imagine, these thoughts heighten Serika's anxiety and leave her feeling stuck. They even stop her from doing some of the things she wants to do.

Similarly, Morgan finds herself saying the following statements to herself throughout the day:

- I'll never get that job, so why bother.

- She obviously hates me.

- I'm so depressed.

- I'll never be able to run a 5k.

Now observe what a shift in diet can do, by simply adding the words "I notice that I feel . . ." or "I notice that I am having the thought that . . ." to these statements. Here they are again, with a slight change of diet:

- I notice that I'm feeling anxious.

- I notice that I'm having the thought that I'm such a loser.

- I notice that I'm thinking to myself how I'm too anxious to raise my hand in class.

- I notice that I'm having the thought that I'll never get that job so why bother.

- I notice I'm thinking to myself that she hates me.

- I notice that I'm feeling depressed right now.

- I notice that I'm having the thought that I'll never be able to run a 5k.

~ Take some of the typical unhealthy thoughts or narratives that you frequently say to yourself and add "I notice that I'm having the thought that" in front of it. How does that shift or change your experience?

~ Bring your awareness into your body and notice the sensations you experience when you say this. What changes when you feed yourself this "I notice" diet versus when you don't?

When we notice and name our feelings as passing emotions and not lasting traits ("I notice that I'm feeling anxious versus I am anxious) and when we observe and name our thoughts for what they are—passing mental events—and not fixed reality, this frees us up in an important way: This isn't the actual movie—it's only the noisy person next to me commenting on the movie! There is a big difference. I am free to take those comments, thoughts, and interpretations more lightly. Just because the noisy person sitting next to me says that I'm too anxious to raise my hand in class doesn't mean that I can't raise my hand in class anyway if I so choose. I may be experiencing self-doubt, but I recognize this is only a story I'm telling myself, not a fixed truth. Yes, I may notice that I'm feeling depressed, but that act of noticing creates the possibility that at some point I may notice that I'm not feeling this way anymore. It is not a fixed, permanent quality about myself (the way "I'm so depressed" suggests).

When we don't realize that we are having negative thoughts or attaching a negative story to our experience, or when we identify with our thoughts as if they are who we are, these thoughts can unknowingly stop us in our tracks. If "I'm such a loser," that is a pretty hopeless situation and there isn't much I can do. I feel physically heavy and stuck. I'm all but doomed. However, if I notice I'm having the thought that I'm a loser, there is a possibility for other options to enter in at some point—and I recognize it's only a thought. I experience more space around me, and a lighter feeling in my body.

The Diet of Present-Moment Thoughts Versus Mental Reruns and Mental Rehearsals

As we've discussed earlier, our mind has a tendency to pull us into past or future ruminations. We can play over and over in our mind something that happened in our recent or distant past, or rehearse over and over something coming up in our future, as part of the default mode of our brain (the dial stuck in an unhelpful place). I like to think of these stuck loops our mind can trap us in as "mental reruns" and "mental rehearsals" (a term I borrowed from psychologist Kellie Edwards [2017]).

As if this wasn't enough, we have the double whammy of that narrator in our head spinning negative, critical and catastrophic tales that get attached to these past and future thoughts. So, we not only re-experience a difficult past situation, but we beat ourselves up over and over with thoughts that we were inadequate in some way. We not only think about what might happen in our future, but we play out all kinds of worst-case scenarios over and over, experiencing them as if they had already happened.

The noisy person at the movie theater, in combination with the tendency of our mind to wander and get stuck in the past or future, creates a negative inner dialogue of ruminations that can be particularly troublesome.

When we get stuck in mental reruns, not only does an event cause us distress at the time that it happens, but it also causes us anguish again—and again . . . and again as we continue to relive it and ruminate about it. Alternatively, when we play scenes over and over in our head of what might happen, we create suffering for ourselves from this imagined event. Even if the event actually happens (for example, dreading a weekend visit from a difficult relative, who turns out in fact to be a difficult guest), we have created double suffering for ourselves. Not only do we experience difficulty when the person is actually at our house for the weekend, but we experience upset during all of the time we are anticipating how bad the weekend is going to be.

Welcome to the world of mental reruns and mental rehearsals—another disguise of the noisy person at the movie theater. When we uncover this disguise, we can use the diet of present moment awareness to bring us back into balance. We can recognize what is happening right here and now, in *this* moment. We can acknowledge our feelings and act skillfully with what is here, without creating double suffering for ourselves.

I find that this thought trap of mental reruns and rehearsals is sneaky and can catch us unaware. I must admit, I tend to fall into mental rehearsals more often than I would like. At a particularly busy time this past spring when I had many commitments and frequent travel plans packed into a span of about a month, I found myself feeling overwhelmed frequently. When I was able to catch the thoughts, they included ones such as "This is going to be a really stressful week" or "How am I going to get everything done?" or "I won't be able to come up for air for another two weeks" or simply rehearsing over and over in my mind everything I had to do, even when it served no purpose to do so. After all, I already had everything planned out and organized.

A friend snapped me back into reality when she pointed out what I was doing. That awareness allowed me to bring myself back into the present moment and feed myself a diet of present-moment thoughts. "Right now, I'm out having dinner with my friends. Can I be with this experience?" "Right now, I'm traveling to New York. Can I be with what is here, without anticipating the stress I *might* be feeling next week?"

Veronica had been struggling with chronic pain for about nine months. She felt pain in her stomach that has no known medical cause. This had become a source of distress for her, and she often disengaged from activities she used to do for fear that the pain might flare up at any point. When Veronica was introduced to the idea of paying attention to the thoughts she was telling herself about her pain, she thought it was a waste of time. She resisted the idea because she was convinced that nothing would help her pain, and since her pain was clearly physical, what did her thoughts have to do with it?

However, with some reluctance, she began to write down her thoughts as they arose around her pain. What she discovered is that she spent a lot of time thinking about the pain that she felt yesterday and earlier this week, and also spent a significant amount of time in her day anticipating her future pain. She did this even at times when her pain was only a minimal "three" on a one-to-ten scale. For example, before getting out of bed, she would play back the previous day's experience and tell herself how bad she felt. Then she would brace herself for what was to come—even though in the actual moment, her level of discomfort was quite tolerable. She also noticed that when she got caught in these reruns and mental rehearsals, her body would tighten and constrict in response to these stressful thoughts.

As she practiced the diet of present-moment awareness, she began to recognize that the thoughts she was having were separate from her present moment experience. For example, she recognized she was anticipating that her pain might become an "eight," but she could bring her awareness back into her body and acknowledge she was feeling a "three". She also practiced sending compassion to herself when she felt fearful and allowed these thoughts to wash over her. One of the things that was most helpful for Veronica about this diet was that she was able to be with whatever she was actually feeling more frequently, instead of being pulled away by her thoughts. Sometimes this meant experiencing high levels of pain and discomfort, but many times, she realized, her pain was at a very tolerable level. She was surprised to see how much her pain actually fluctuated during the day. She also stopped predicting when she *might* feel pain, and started doing more things that she enjoyed that she had been avoiding. Knowing that she could always go home if her pain level became too high was helpful, but being willing to dive in meant that many times she was fine and did not have to miss out on her life.

An On-the-Spot Strategy for Stepping Out of Mental Reruns and Rehearsals

The next time you notice yourself feeling stressed, distressed, or stuck in unhelpful ruminations, stop and ask yourself:

~ How much of what I am feeling is actually connected with what is happening right now?

~ How much of my upset is related to replaying something that happened in the past or an anticipated or imagined future event?

~ What would be here now if I chose to just be present with what is unfolding today?

The Diet of Self-Compassion Versus Shame and Blame

We often can be quite critical and harsh with ourselves in a way that we would never be with anyone else. We say things to ourselves, like "I'm so stupid" or "I'm such an idiot." When we make mistakes we might call ourselves a "loser" or a "failure." These kinds of global statements attack us at the core of our character and who we are. In addition, we often think of ourselves as defective, broken, less than, unworthy, or even unlovable.

These are the stories that we attach to our experiences of loss, heartbreak, disappointment or hurt. Even the most successful people often think of themselves at times as phonies, imposters and inadequate. This is a syndrome we tend to fall into on account of being human. The problem is when this kind of language and thinking goes beneath the surface of our consciousness and becomes part of our belief system, it can be destructive to our well-being. When we begin to pay attention, we may realize that this kind of thinking makes up the staple of our diet. As Tara Brach (2013) suggests, we can then bring loving presence and mindful awareness and inquiry to these limiting beliefs about ourselves, to help us step out of our fear-based conditioning and dissolve these stuck patterns.

Here are a few steps we can take to address and correct this unhealthy diet:

1. We can think about the situation through the eyes of another person, such as a good friend. If this were happening to a good friend, would we say these words, or would we use a more compassionate approach? Or, alternatively, how might a good friend respond to us in this situation?

2. Instead of making our language broad and generalized, we can make it specific to the circumstances. This is a powerful way to shift us out of shame and blame and into accountability and ownership. It allows us to take responsibility for what is ours to change, but not to attack our character and the core of who we are). Researcher Brene Brown makes an important distinction between shame (I am bad) versus guilt (I did something bad). The first is an attack on our character that leaves us feeling hopeless. The second is a specific statement of something we did wrong that allows for accountability, hope and change (Brown, 2017).

3. Instead of trying to get rid of the noisy person in the theater, we can turn and look at them with compassion. We can

recognize the scared, angry or hurt parts of ourselves in them, extend some kindness and recognize that we, too, are human. We can do this while choosing not to accept their words as gospel. They are only the words of someone feeling scared, angry, hurt, etc.

Tip: One way to shift from shame and blame to self-compassion is to refocus our attention from our thoughts to our bodies and just be with the physical sensations that are there. We will explore this further in the next chapter.

Ahmed had been dating his girlfriend seriously for two years when she suddenly ended the relationship without much warning. She told Ahmed that he was just not the right one for her and she needed to move on. Ahmed was heartbroken. As if this loss wasn't bad enough, Ahmed began to attach a story to the breakup that went something like this: "I'm an idiot for losing her. I'm defective and unlovable. No one will ever want to be with me. I am not worthy of another relationship." Now he was no longer just sad, but depressed as well. The noisy person at the movie theater strikes again.

With some practice, Ahmed was able to recognize how his own thinking and his perception of the situation contributed to his intense distress. He worked on feeding himself a different diet. He imagined this situation happening to a friend and realized he would perceive the situation very differently. He wouldn't think of his friend as an idiot, blame him for the breakup, or consider him unworthy of future relationships. He would feel compassion for his friend for experiencing this loss. He would see his friend as lovable and worthy of another relationship. Taking this perspective helped him gain a sense of how to look at his situation with greater self-compassion. Instead of saying "I'm an idiot for losing her" he tried out "I'm hurting very deeply that she left." Changing these phrases allowed him to acknowledge and experience greater compassion for himself and what he was going through. Feeling compassion for others during difficult times was easy, but it felt very foreign to do this for himself.

When Ahmed looked further at the break up, he realized that just because his girlfriend was unhappy in the relationship did not make him defective, unlovable or unworthy. These implied global, unchangeable flaws in his character and that didn't fit the circumstances. Instead, he was able to change this narrative: He was not the right person for her. There were qualities she was looking for in a person that he did not have. There were also some problems in their communication that needed improvement. He could recognize some of this was on him, and it was something he could work to improve in future relationships.

This change in diet didn't take away the grief and sadness Ahmed felt over the loss of the relationship, but it did shift his feelings of shame and blame and helped him cope more effectively with his loss.

Miriam, an elementary school teacher, had a particularly challenging week with her own two children, ages three and five, who had multiple meltdowns each day when they came home from preschool. In addition, Miriam was recovering from a foot injury and experiencing some pain and immobility. Toward the end of the week, when her three-year-old spilled her cereal all over the floor, Miriam lost her temper. She yelled and screamed, resulting in both daughters becoming quite upset. After she apologized to the girls and calmed them down, she began beating herself up emotionally, telling herself she was a terrible mother, a failure and that she didn't deserve to be a teacher or work with children. Normally, she did not think twice when she talked to herself this way. Often, she did not even realize she was talking to herself in this way, but later she would then lie awake at night unable to sleep because she felt so badly.

This time she heard the harshness of her own words. She thought about several of her friends with small children and remembered that she was not the only mother who ever had a meltdown with her children. She recognized that if this happened to one of her friends, she would certainly not consider her a horrible mother. When Miriam was able to change her diet to make it more specific, it sounded something like this: "I'm really upset with myself that I yelled and screamed at my daughter today. I don't like acting like that and there was a much better way I could have handled the situation. It upset my daughter and that was hard to see." When we make our language specific to the circumstances, it switches the focus from something defective about us as a person, to a *behavior* we are upset about. Saying this to herself gave her more room to cope with the situation. Being compassionate with herself did not mean that she approved of her behavior, but it did allow her to recognize that she is human. It encouraged her to develop some strategies that could be used in the future if she felt overwhelmed and close to the breaking point again.

Pay attention to the diet you feed yourself— it matters more than you realize!

One very wet and rainy spring, we had a bit of a mudslide on the side of our house where one of our cars was parked. What was usually firm ground turned into a muddy mess. When my daughter tried to back the car out, the wheels spun in the mud. The harder she tried to back out, the deeper the wheels dug into the mud and the more stuck the car became. We had to steer the car in a completely different direction to disengage it from where it was trapped.

When we tell ourselves unhelpful stories and inaccurate thoughts or repeat self-critical words over and over, we carve pathways in our mind like the car stuck in the mud. It becomes easier and easier to return to these negative thought tracks the more we repeat them, and harder to escape the traps we've created for ourselves. Once we recognize we are spinning our wheels in our negative narratives, we can make a choice to carve out a new pathway by feeding ourselves a more nourishing diet. When we unhook from our thinking, and recognize our thoughts as separate from our experience, we create greater freedom and choice.

Interestingly, brain science research has shown that practicing mindfulness meditation can help with this unhooking process. The more we practice observing our thoughts, the more the part of our brain that is pulled into narrative and self-referential thinking can unhook from the part of the brain that processes present-moment sensory experiences. This allows us to experience what is happening without being so pulled into and driven by our stories (Segal, 2016).

Once we can identify the many disguises of the noisy person at the movie theater, we have already taken an important step toward avoiding the unhelpful thought loop. Life is challenging enough without adding additional suffering through our unhelpful, inaccurate, and self-critical stories. A healthy diet, on the other hand, makes us more resilient to cope with whatever is thrown our way.

Practices

The Pie Chart Exercise

- Begin to pay attention to the diet you feed yourself every day. Do you tend to have a well-balanced diet of healthy and accurate thoughts, or do you feed yourself unrealistic thoughts, self-critical thoughts, mental reruns, etc. Each person will have a diet that looks different.

- Take a typical day and make a pie chart illustrating how much of the time you spend in each of the following listed below. (This will give you an idea of what you most need to work on and what is working well for you.) You will end up with the pie divided into eight pieces, but the size of each piece will reflect how much time you tend to spend in each kind of diet throughout the day.

  * Accurate and Helpful Thinking

  * Distorted Thinking

  * Self-critical Thinking/Shame and Blame

  * Self-Compassion

  * Present-Moment Thinking

  * Mental Reruns/ Mental Rehearsals

  * Noticing Thoughts as Just Thoughts

  * Being Dragged Down the River by Thoughts

- Make note of which unhealthy diets you most get pulled into, and set a small goal for yourself to catch these thoughts as much as possible over the next week. Notice what happens as you become more aware of the diet you feed yourself.

Unhooking from Our Thoughts

Think of the word "unhook" and use the following acronym when you notice you are feeding yourself an unhealthy diet:

Understand that I am not my thoughts (they are just mental creations of my mind).

Notice when unhelpful thoughts arise.

Hold my thoughts lightly—don't give them more weight than they deserve.

Observe my thoughts from the bank of the river.

Offer kindness to the part of me that wants to believe every thought as true.

Know that I can choose a more helpful narrative if I want.

Meditation to Nourish Ourselves

Allow yourself to get into a comfortable position where you can use this script to guide you through a short visualization/meditation. Begin by taking a moment to feel your feet on the ground and notice the sensation of support beneath you. Bring your awareness into your body and begin to take several slow, deep breaths, following each breath as it comes in and each breath as it goes out.

When you are ready, call up a typical situation where the noisy person at the movie theater might appear during your day. Imagine that you could watch this scene play out before you. Notice what the noisy person is saying to you. Rather than getting swept away by these words, see if you might simply notice this diet of thoughts he or she is feeding you, from a bit of a distance, and watch these words pass by. You might even imagine saying to yourself, "Oh, that's just the noisy person at the movie theater." If you like, you might send yourself some compassion for whatever is difficult about the situation at hand, without getting pulled into the narrative of the noisy person at the movie theater. If there is an opening to do so, see if there are more accurate words or thoughts that you might feed yourself that are more helpful and specific to the situation.

Feel free to go through additional situations if you like. When you are ready, bring your awareness back into the room.

As you go through your week, practice catching the noisy person at the movie theater, noticing his/her disguises, and practice feeding yourself a healthier diet of accurate and self-compassionate thoughts. Writing these new and more helpful narratives down as you go through your day can be immensely helpful.

CHAPTER FOUR

The Door: Befriending the Darkness to Become Fully Alive

AFTER MY DAUGHTER WAS BORN, I began to experience a great deal of deep grief about the loss of my mother that I had not been aware was there. Becoming a mother, and not having my own mother alive and with me at this time brought up emotions that I had not fully dealt with in my earlier years. When I became pregnant two years later with my second child, I experienced fears about whether I would remain healthy and have a normal delivery, given the toxemia and emergency delivery I had with my first child. I had become aware of the risks and this frightened me because these were aspects of pregnancy over which I had no control.

This sense of not having control over certain things in my life was especially triggering for me because of the traumatic and sudden way that my mother died when I was fifteen. Her death was the ultimate loss of control and it left me with a feeling that at any moment, something scary or devastating could happen. On one hand, I coped with these fears by putting my energy into controlling the things I could and living the fullest life possible by taking care of my health and well-being. I ate healthy foods, exercised regularly, surrounded myself with caring friends, threw myself into my studies and did well in college and graduate school. But this only got me so far. I was all too aware that on the other end of things was this fragility of life dangling over my head. The nature of my daughter's birth was a first-hand reminder that scary things could happen unexpectedly. The time between the birth of my daughter and the birth of my son gave me an opportunity to come face-to-face with many emotions—vulnerability, fear, grief, and sadness— that I had been keeping at bay.

Tool Three: The Door

One of the greatest challenges I have found in my own life is learning how to be present to the "darker" emotions that are so much easier to push away. I have certainly experienced the "finger trap dilemma" first hand, as I have noticed my own inclination to avoid discomfort. Through the guidance of some wonderful therapists, and the practice of mindfulness, I learned to turn toward the discomfort, instead of away from it. This leaning in and befriending my sadness, grief and fear was one of the greatest gifts to myself, and brought with it much personal growth and freedom. I have seen this befriending of difficult emotions transform the lives of many of my patients as well.

Joseph Campbell, in his book, *The Power of Myth*, wrote: "People say that what we're all seeking is a meaning for life. I don't think that's what we're really seeking… I think that what we're seeking is an experience of being alive. " One of the things I have experienced in both my personal and professional life is that we learn to awaken and become fully alive by embracing the whole of our experience in all of its imperfections. We awaken as we learn to be present to the joys *and* the suffering (sorrows) in our lives, as we grow our own strengths, and accept our own weaknesses and vulnerabilities. When we can be present with whatever is arising— even the difficult emotions—we open up to the whole of what life has to offer. Rather than trying to swim upstream, we let the current carry us to safe ground. As we awaken, we learn that safety lies in our own open hearts.

Using the Door

I have been fascinated by the neuroscience research and the research on mindfulness that has emerged to support this idea that turning towards our internal experiences (even those that involve emotional or physical discomfort), rather than avoiding or pushing them away, is a good thing for our well-being. When we turn toward our cravings, we are less likely to engage in addictive behaviors; when we turn toward our physical pain, we are less likely to be trapped in cycles of chronic pain; when we turn toward our sadness, we are less likely to be stuck in depression; and when we turn toward our anxiety, we are less likely to be paralyzed by it and will find it easier to bear (Halliwell, 2017). As you may recall, however, this runs counter to our evolutionary tendency to avoid pain and seek pleasure. So, we need a tool to help with this finger-trap dilemma. How can we learn to turn toward discomfort?

I love open water swimming, mostly in lakes, but sometimes in the ocean. I bought a wetsuit years ago to compete in triathlons, and I still use it occasionally. Often the waters that I swim in are calm, but sometimes they can be rather rough, with choppy waves and white caps. When I put on the wetsuit, it gives me added buoyancy so that I can swim into the waves and let the water toss me about, knowing that I will stay on the surface. While it takes a lot more effort to swim in the waves than in calm waters, it is reassuring to know that I can experience the rougher waters and ride the waves without being swept away.

So how do we learn to be with difficult emotions without running the other way? How do we allow ourselves to be vulnerable and experience the ups *and* downs of life while not losing ourselves? This is where the door comes in. The door is a powerful tool and metaphor for learning to make a space for difficult emotions and to be with them in a compassionate way. When we open the door, when we know we can allow in our sadness, grief, anxiety, fear, anger, frustration, disappointment or hurt, we also open ourselves more widely to the richness that life has to offer, and we develop greater resilience to bounce back from adversities large and small.

When I sit with my patients who are experiencing difficult emotions, we sometimes imagine that they are opening the door and welcoming the emotions in, to come and have a seat somewhere in the room (something I learned from some very wonderful therapists during my own therapy). They can picture this seat as close or as far away from them as they like. From this perspective, they can take a gentle and curious look at what is there.

Often people will picture their emotions as having some kind of color, shape or form; sometimes they envision their emotions as cartoon characters, or as younger parts of themselves. Part of the practice is simply to accept whatever arrives, and to be with it in a compassionate way, the way you might sit with a good friend. This is a new experience for most people. Who *wants* to let anxiety in the door? Who *wants* to welcome in sadness? Having been on the other end as a patient, and having experienced this opening of the door many times myself in therapy, I know there is something healing about learning to sit with sadness or anger or anxiety this way. Rather than fighting to hold the door closed and keep everything on the other side out, there is a freedom in opening the door and embracing the whole of our human experience—the pleasant and unpleasant parts alike. As Tara Brach teaches, it is learning to say "yes" to life with an open-hearted presence, even in its most challenging moments, that allows us to discover "true refuge" within ourselves (Brach, 2013).

When we can let in whatever arrives at the door, and see it from a bit of a distance in the chair across from us, we can take a curious look and explore what is there. We can practice mindfulness of body sensations and emotions and offer non-judgment to whatever shows up in the room. It need not feel pleasant. Knowing that we have the capacity to bear whatever is there, that we can envision a room large enough to hold the whole of our experience and the whole of ourselves, we can accept and meet life where we are.

There are three steps in using the door as a tool: 1. First is being willing to open the door and invite in whatever is there—allowing it to come and have a seat in the room. This is the opposite of resisting. 2. The second part is to take a curious look at what is there and to simply be with whatever you are experiencing as it unfolds without needing it to be different than what it is. This encourages acceptance. This doesn't mean, however, that you need to like what is there, or that you need to act on it. I might accept that I am feeling angry and be willing to explore this experience of anger in my body even though it is uncomfortable. Allowing myself to explore the anger does not mean acting out my anger. There is an important distinction between feeling emotions in our bodies and taking actions through our behaviors. 3. The third part is to sit with whatever walks in the door the way you would sit with a good friend, with compassion and kindness. I wouldn't tell my friend that they are stupid for feeling angry or should just snap out of it. I wouldn't tell my friend that I only want to be around them when they are in a good mood, and then abandon them every time they are sad, upset or experiencing pain in some way. I would listen with openness and acknowledge the difficulty of what they are experiencing. Note that in the previous chapter we touched upon how to bring self-compassion into what we are thinking, to replace self-critical thoughts. Here we will focus on how to bring self-compassion to what we are feeling.

Below are some examples of how you might use the door and each of its three parts.

Please be aware that while the door is a tool we can use in our daily lives, when we are working with very intense emotions, or traumas, it is important to work with the guidance of a skilled mental health professional.

Step 1: Developing a willingness to open the door.

Sometimes opening the door can feel difficult, foreign, or perhaps even scary, especially if it has been closed for a long time and we are used to keeping it shut. This might be the case if we have avoided certain activities or aspects of our life for quite some time in order to ward off anxious feelings, or if we are masters at pushing away sadness. We also might be so busy in our lives that we don't make time to sit and feel what is there. For many people, it is much easier to attend to other people's feelings than their own. Whatever your experience is with opening the door, it is helpful to remind yourself that you are not alone. It is part of our human experience to steer clear of discomfort. It is also important to know that you get to control when and how much you open the door. Sometimes opening it a little bit at a time can be a helpful approach, especially if more intense emotions are there.

~

~   Ask yourself what emotion(s) you have the most difficulty expressing? What emotions do you most often push away?

Jovana (from Chapter Two) you may recall, works as a nurse, has two small children (one with special needs), and an aging mother who lives with her. She spends much of her time caretaking and is very good at it. However, she finds herself irritable and overwhelmed frequently, and her response to this is to push through, ignore it, and muster on. She had started to use mindful pauses at the beginning, middle and end of her day and was finding this helpful. After practicing with these mindful pauses, she decided also to try and use a mindful pause when she noticed signs of difficult emotions arising, such as feeling irritated or overwhelmed. After a frustrating interchange with her mother, she walked away and took a few minutes for herself. She imagined opening the door and was surprised to see sadness coming in. She recognized that some of her irritability at her mom was really sadness about her mom aging and beginning to show signs of memory loss. Seeing this helped her to acknowledge, "This is difficult," and to offer some kindness to herself. It also gave her an opening to reach out to some friends, who were dealing with similar challenges.

At another point, after she had put her children to bed, she felt depleted and exhausted. Taking a few minutes to notice and be with the feelings she was experiencing, she became aware of anger that she hadn't been aware of directly. Normally, she would dismiss this and move on (having learned from an early age to put her anger away), but she chose to notice it further and let it be there. She recognized that she was upset at her husband for not helping out more with the children, yet she never said anything to him about this. Acknowledging the feelings were there, she realized it might be important to talk with him before the resentment built up in unhealthy ways.

Fernando was afraid to fly, and as you may recall from Chapter Two, his fear stopped him from visiting his family across the country. His fear also stopped him from dating and from driving on the highway. Opening "the door" for Fernando involved working with a therapist to help him take small steps to sit with his discomfort, in order to fully live the life that he wanted. Fernando made a hierarchy of feared experiences, from least to most uncomfortable. For example, one of the things lower on his list regarding dating was signing up for an online dating service, followed by reaching out and messaging someone, followed by calling them, followed by going on a date. In terms of flying, his hierarchy included going to an airport and watching planes take off (which raised only a little anxiety for him), to experiencing increasing levels of anxiety by flying from Boston to New York to visit a friend, to very high anxiety flying on a six-hour trip. Identifying small steps that he was willing to take despite experiencing some discomfort allowed Fernando to gain the confidence he needed for more challenging steps. Each time he was able to open the door and do what he wanted to do despite some discomfort, he experienced a feeling of freedom knowing he did not need to stay trapped behind his fears.

When my son was in middle school and high school, he repeatedly sustained minor injuries of broken bones—usually his fingers or wrist—that stopped him from playing his beloved sports. After one of the last injuries he had in high school, I recall taking him to the doctor where my son learned he would miss most of his junior varsity season of soccer, which he deeply loved. After the appointment, he got in the car and sobbed. I had not seen him break down like that since he was a little boy, and it was a deep, painful cry as he made contact with his tremendous sorrow. Yet after he allowed himself to fully experience this pain—once he could be fully present to it and accept what was there—he was able to move forward in an amazingly resilient way.

Step 2: Taking a curious look at whatever walks in the door.

Observing what we are feeling from a place of mindfulness (paying attention, on purpose, in the present moment, without judgment) can help us cope with whatever is there. It can sometimes help to name what we are feeling ("Oh, that is hurt coming in; that is jealousy; that is anger").

As simple as this sounds, we often don't pay attention to the nuances of what we are feeling and consequently, important information gets lost along the way. It can also be beneficial to see our emotional "visitors" as temporary guests. Adding the phrase, "in this moment," to the statement, "I am feeling stress, anger or hurt," can help us be with what is there without feeling overwhelmed. Other things you might say to yourself as you look at who comes through your door, include: "Can I be with what is here? Can I allow myself to notice how this is showing up in my body and in my thoughts? If this feeling or part of me could talk, what might it say?"

Tamako had a strong love-hate relationship with her mother. Her mother had a difficult upbringing and, as a result, her mother had strong unmet needs that she sought to fill through her daughter, not always in the healthiest of ways. Her mother was unable to meet Tamako's emotional needs as a young girl and, as a result, Tamako grew up closing off these needs and adopting a strong stance of independence and self-sufficiency. When she found out her mother was dying of cancer, Tamako's first inclination was to avoid having to deal with her mother and her illness as much as possible.

As she was able to become comfortable with her own mixed emotions and to sit mindfully with the uncomfortable feelings in her body, she became in touch with her own unmet needs and the feelings of loss and sadness that she had pushed away for many years. She was able to recognize that the strong, independent part of her also longed for the loving, attentive mother that she never had. Allowing herself to connect with these feelings and name them, she was able to begin to reach out to her mother. Increasingly, she began to recognize her mother's imperfections but she was also able to open herself up to what her mother could offer. Being able to open the door allowed Tamako to be with her mother during the time of her death, and to come to peace with their relationship.

A number of years ago, one of my children was prescribed a medication with many potentially serious, even toxic, side effects that they needed to be on for a long period of time. The possible consequences terrified me. I experienced extreme anxiety prior to the start of this medication and resisted exploring my own emotions for quite some time. Then one day, I allowed myself to come face to face with my fears, to open the door and take a look at what was there.

When I finally was present with my emotions, I discovered that it wasn't so much putting my child on this medication that terrified me (though that was a concern), but it was my realization that as much as I hold onto the illusion of control, there are no guarantees in life. I can't protect my children and keep them one hundred percent safe. Coming face to face with that deep loss and sadness about the fragility of life, and allowing myself to feel it, helped me to move forward with greater resilience—and even ease—having named what was truly underneath it all.

Step 3: Giving the gift of compassion.

Besides our evolutionary tendencies to push away uncomfortable feelings, many of us have been conditioned to judge our own emotions in negative ways. We often learn or come to believe that if we show sadness, it is a sign of weakness; that we are a bad person if we feel anger or jealousy; that we should "move on" when we experience loss, that we are unstable if we show vulnerability. When we come face to face with difficult emotions, we often tell ourselves to buck up, pull it together, stop being so silly, or what's wrong with me that I'm feeling this way.

Remember that one of the core components of mindfulness, besides intentionally paying attention, is to bring a quality of non-judgmental awareness to our experience. If a good friend or a small child were feeling sadness, fear, anger or some other difficult emotion, we would probably listen openly and perhaps put an arm around them or extend a hand. Yet when it comes to ourselves, we often don't learn to do that. When we can practice mindfulness in combination with self-kindness and a recognition of our common humanity (the fact that we all suffer as human beings), we cultivate self-compassion, a quality that has been linked to psychological well-being (Neff and Germer, 2017).

Imagine for a moment sitting with a good friend. Think about how you might extend a gesture of compassion if that person were having a difficult time. What would your body language be like? How might you listen? What sensations would you feel around your heart (e.g., perhaps a quality of openness).

Now imagine you were sitting with that good friend and you were the one going through a hard time. Picture that person extending compassion towards you. What might they say or do? What words would you find comforting or soothing? Chances are, they would not be telling you to cut it out, that you shouldn't be feeling this way, or giving advice about how to snap out of it. Perhaps instead they might say, "That sounds really hard. I'm here for you." Or perhaps they might simply extend a hand.

When we can learn to sit mindfully with our own emotions, and bring compassion to whatever we are experiencing, it is as if we have become that caring friend, sitting with ourselves. Learning to be there for ourselves, through the positive moments as well as the painful ones, can be tremendously healing.

Joe grew up in an alcoholic home where his father shouted at him and called him mean names whenever his father drank too much. While Joe became successful as an adult, he carried around a feeling that something was wrong with him. He tended to interpret situations by personalizing them and seeing himself as inadequate, even when this was not how others saw things. In response, he would sometimes react out of anger, or shut down and withdraw; an automatic response he had learned as a way to protect himself. It never occurred to Joe to feel compassion towards himself in these situations, as this was something foreign to him. However, Joe was a very loyal friend and husband, and knew how to be compassionate when others were in pain. Joe began to pay attention to the times when he was triggered and would become angry or withdraw.

On one particular day when he drove into a parking lot, he took a parking spot not realizing someone else had been waiting for it. The person in the other car made a frustrated gesture and gave him an angry look before pulling away. Joe could feel himself starting to withdraw and shut down, feeling a sense of shame and inadequacy for doing something "wrong." Instead of pushing the feelings away and shutting down, however, he practiced opening the door and acknowledging what was there.

First, he told himself that what he was feeling was difficult and he acknowledged he was struggling. Once he did this, he was able to recognize the younger part of himself that was reacting; not his adult self, but the young boy who felt terrible every time his father yelled at him. Intellectually, he recognized that he was not a bad person for accidentally taking another person's parking spot, but the younger part of him felt a great deal of shame and guilt. Naming this hurt, he imagined sitting with this younger version of himself, telling him that he understood how painful it was to grow up with his volatile and unpredictable father. He imagined extending a hand and telling his younger self that he was not to blame for his father's behavior.

This was a powerful experience for Joe to learn how to be mindful and experience self-compassion when he was feeling difficult emotions. A part of him relaxed as he did this, and he no longer felt the need to withdraw and close himself off at that moment.

Susan applied for a job that she wanted very badly. When she didn't get it, she felt deeply upset. When she found out a close colleague with less experience was offered the job, she became even more upset. When upsetting things happened, Susan tended to brush these feelings away and put on a happy face. She didn't like being vulnerable and she wanted others to think that things were no big deal. She tried to convince herself of this as well, and the last thing she wanted to do was wallow in her own self-pity. While she typically did a good job of pushing these feelings away, she would often experience headaches or other physical symptoms. When Susan decided to practice using "the door" tool, she recognized she would need to make space for some of these uncomfortable emotions.

In this particular situation, she allowed herself to name her disappointment at not getting the job, and the jealousy she felt toward the person who got the offer. She put her hand on her heart and felt the heaviness in her chest as she told herself it was okay and normal to feel these emotions. She imagined sitting with a friend going through something similar and simply being there for her without trying to fix it. To her surprise, sending herself this self-compassion did not cause her to wallow in self-pity, but in fact allowed her to feel more inner strength and resilience. It allowed her painful emotions to move through her more easily, without getting stuck.

I don't know much about boating, but I will leave you with one more metaphor that I hope may be helpful. During the times when I have been out in a motor boat on the open water, I have been told that whenever there is a wave coming, steer the boat straight into it, hitting it perpendicular. This seems a little counterintuitive to me, because my first inclination is to turn and try to get away in whatever way I can. But I can understand that there is more stability heading straight into the wave, rather than hitting it parallel where it could more easily flip the boat over onto its side.

Life is filled with waves. We can't avoid them. The best we can do is learn to navigate so that we stay afloat and know how to handle them, without letting our fear of the waves prevent us from getting out on the boat and enjoying all the adventures that it has to offer.

Suggested Practices

Using the Door in Daily Life

As you go through your day, notice when a difficult emotion arises (perhaps disappointment, frustration, anger or sadness). When you have a chance, set aside a few minutes to sit quietly and be with what you are feeling. Think about and practice the three steps of using the door (again, remembering that if you have experienced a trauma or are experiencing very intense emotions, only do this with the guidance of a skilled mental health professional):

1. Be willing to open the door and take a peek at what is there. See if you might let it in and offer it a seat somewhere in the room. Practice turning toward what is there, instead of turning away from it.

2. Take a curious look at what is there. Name it. Drop your awareness into your body and experience any sensations that arise. You might picture riding the waves, knowing your emotions are passing events that build, crest, and eventually dissipate. Picture an anchor and imagine holding onto the anchor as the waves come and go, or imagine meeting each wave with the safety of a wetsuit, or surf board, or life jacket.

As you take a look at the emotion that is present in the room, you might notice if it has a shape or a color or takes on a particular image. You might note how much space it takes up and how it changes over time as you sit with it. You might be curious about whether this emotion feels directly connected with a situation occurring now, or whether it reminds you of emotions you may have experienced at an earlier time in your life.

3. Bring compassion to whatever you are experiencing. Say kind words to the part of you that is experiencing these emotions, or say something supportive that you might say to a friend going through a similar difficult situation. If you prefer, you don't need to say any words, but just let yourself know that you are there for yourself.

On the following page is an acronym to help you use the tool of The Door as you go through the day:

Drop your attention into your body. Notice what physical sensations are present.

Open the door and allow space for whatever emotions you are feeling to be there. Send some breath to places in your body where those emotions are being held.

Observe whatever arises from a non-judgmental and open place.

Reach out to any parts of you that are hurting and extend compassion and kindness.

Opening the Door Through Writing

Some people find that writing can be a helpful tool to put words to emotions that might otherwise remain out of awareness. The next time you find yourself experiencing a challenging emotion, set aside a few minutes to write down the answers to these questions:

What is the emotion you are feeling? Is it sadness, grief, despair, frustration, anger, rage, disappointment, irritation? Be as specific as possible.

If the emotion could talk freely and didn't have to worry about being judged in any way, what would it say? What would this emotion say about its beliefs about you and the world? What might it say about its needs? Write as much as comes to mind, until you experience a feeling of completeness and being fully heard.

Imagine yourself as a compassionate friend or caregiver. How might you respond to the emotion, to validate and acknowledge what has been expressed? Try not to "fix" the problem, offer advice, or criticize or judge what was said. It is O.K. to offer some heartfelt wisdom, but only if it feels validating and self-compassionate.

CHAPTER FIVE

The Magnifying Glass:
Finding the Hidden Joys

WHEN MY BELOVED GRANDMA MAE was well into her nineties, she lived in an assisted-living facility about three-and-a-half hours from my house. At that time, my life was extremely busy juggling two small children (not literally, though it felt like it), working in my outpatient practice, and training for triathlons in my spare time. I loved my grandmother and wanted to make sure I saw her as regularly as I could, so I set aside a Saturday when I could drive down and spend the day with her.

I left my house early and was relieved that the traffic was light, which meant all the more time to spend with her. I arrived eagerly after the long drive, excited to see her. When I walked into her room, the one thing happened that I had not anticipated—she was fast asleep! I tried to rouse her by saying hello loudly, but she didn't budge. I then tried to gently put my hand on her shoulder, but she was in a deep sleep and still didn't rouse. I didn't have the heart to wake her by shaking her more vigorously, so I waited . . . and waited some more.

At first it was no big deal. After a bit of time elapsed, my mind started to fill with negative thoughts and they increased as time passed: "I can't believe I drove all this way and now she's sleeping. What if she doesn't wake up for a long time? Then I'll hardly have any time with her. What if I drove seven hours for nothing?" Realizing I was getting worked up and pulled into negativity, I did the only thing I could think of. I sat on the edge of her bed and began meditating, following my breath in and out. After a short while, I became aware not only of my own breath, but of hers. As I listened to her breathing I was overcome with a feeling that one might have watching a sleeping child. I became very aware of her presence, and I began to feel the love and warmth of being in her company. My heart filled with a sense of gratitude, and I felt a deep connection to my grandmother. As I became more and more present, I was aware of a feeling of satisfaction within. I felt in that moment that even if she kept sleeping and we only had a very brief time together, there was a sense of completeness in being with her.

My grandmother did wake up a short time later and we had a memorable visit. But that experience helped me recognize how easy it would have been for me to get caught in negativity by focusing on the time that we didn't have. In doing so, I would have completely missed this opportunity to be present with her in this unexpected way. It also reminded me that each day is made up of opportunities for this kind of presence; opportunities to savor what is right in front of us that we could so easily miss (and often do). It made me reflect on the question of how to take the ordinary and even mundane moments of our lives and transform them into something extraordinary.

Tool Four: The Magnifying Glass

Why do we need a magnifying glass if we already have a flashlight? The flashlight helps us see whatever is there, but the magnifying glass helps us to enlarge the positive aspects of our world that we might otherwise overlook. Remember the Velcro problem that makes it more likely that we will notice and grab onto the negatives in our day, and let the positives slip away? The magnifying glass is a tool we can carry with us to ensure that we don't miss those small, positive moments in our day which, when added together, can create greater joy and meaning in our lives.

At any given moment, when we look around us or go through our day, there could be a hundred things to focus on. As I am sitting here right now getting ready to meditate, I can focus on all the weeds growing in my yard, or I can relish the beauty of the azalea that is just starting to bloom. Now, there is nothing wrong with noticing the weeds and perhaps pulling them if I choose, but when I do this at the cost of missing the azalea, I also miss that moment of peace, beauty and calmness that goes along with taking in the azalea. I can focus my attention on the frustrating phone call I just had with my insurance company, or the loving glance from my daughter as she walks into the house. These are all choices I get to make moment to moment.

An important point here is that the magnifying glass is not about burying our head in the sand when we have real problems or challenges in front of us. There are difficult things that may require our attention and uncomfortable emotions that may need to be acknowledged (as we learned to do using the tool "the door"). However, the magnifying glass reminds us not to miss the small jewels right before us that we might otherwise overlook.

My idea of a magnifying glass as a tool, and many of the practices in this chapter, were in part inspired by several courses I took with neuropsychologist Rick Hanson (2016). Much of his teaching and writing emphasizes the importance of "taking in the good" and savoring these small, beneficial moments throughout our day. Taking in these moments not only can create greater well-being, but also can create lasting changes in our brains. Dr. Hanson explains that many people miss an important step of this process as they go through their day. Even if people notice good things in their day, they often miss the opportunity to "install" these experiences. It is not only important to notice good moments, but equally important to let them "sink in;" let the good feelings be absorbed and savored as a feeling state within our bodies. Doing this for twenty to thirty seconds or more repeatedly over time can help to turn passing states into lasting traits (Hanson, 2016).

When we notice something positive and allow ourselves to experience this positivity in our bodies, we are activating the mind-body connection. Rather than just having a passing thought—"Those are beautiful flowers" or "I'm happy that I had time to stop for my favorite coffee"— we pause to take this experience into our bodies and notice what shows up as we do so. The magnifying glass invites us to notice a positive experience (or even a positive quality in ourselves), and then bring our awareness into our bodies and experience this positive emotional state as a *felt sense* and not just as an intellectual knowing. We then have the opportunity to magnify and expand whatever feelings of appreciation, gratitude, or positivity might be there. We can use the magnifying glass to highlight something in our outer environment (e.g., a situation, an experience, an object that we perceive through our senses), as well as the accompanying aspects in our inner environment (the world of our thoughts, feelings and sensations).

The magnifying glass can bring greater moments of joy or positivity into our day, which can add up over time in significant ways. It can also help us bolster our resilience and it can be a buffer against stress. When we are caught in negativity and focused on what is not going well in our day, the addition of one more negative thing can be the tipping point that sends us spiraling out of control, or plummeting into the deep hole of irritability, stress or overwhelm. The other day, I received an unexplained electric bill whose cost was through the roof. I was mulling over this bill and, quite honestly, letting it get the better of me, when I noticed that someone had left dirty dishes in the sink. Normally this might not have triggered me, but because I was already caught up in negativity about the bill, I flew off the handle and overreacted.

In contrast, another time I started my day by focusing on feelings of gratitude and connection. Not far along into the morning, I got a flat tire on the way to the train station to pick up relatives. I had to wait for over an hour to get my tire changed. I was delayed picking up my visitors and it threw a curve ball into the entire day. I was not ruffled at all by this but quite enjoyed my time waiting, and felt appreciation for the kind police officer who helped me back the car into a safe spot to wait for AAA to come and change my tire. If I had been caught in a spiral of negativity, that same flat tire probably would have triggered a very different reaction.

So when we build moments of positivity into our day through the use of the magnifying glass, we have more reserves to draw on when we hit those unexpected bumps in the road. Barbara Fredrickson's (2009) research on positivity highlights this and elaborates on the resources available to us when we access positive emotions: better health, greater social connection, increased ability to attend to the present moment, greater self-acceptance and a sense of purpose.

There are many different ways to bring the magnifying glass into our day. One way we can do this is to notice what is already in front of us by focusing on unfolding events in our day, or finding the "jewels" that are already present (Hanson, 2018). Additionally, however, we can also focus on and appreciate positive qualities within ourselves as they appear throughout the day (e.g., our patience, perseverance, determination, etc.). Another way we can use the magnifying glass is to engage our mind and imagination to call up *past* positive experiences and their accompanying positive feeling states. For example, we might think about a time when we experienced a deep sense of calmness or peace, and intentionally recall that experience in *this* moment. When we do this, we experience all the benefits of being in a positive emotional state, including the brain changes that occur when doing so. We can also use the magnifying glass to find positives within challenging situations, to help reframe how we are looking at something and what aspect of a situation we choose to focus on. So we can hover the magnifying glass in many different ways. Below are some illustrations of how to use the magnifying glass in these ways.

Magnifying What is in Front of Us

Using the magnifying glass to focus on what is already in front of us involves nothing more than training ourselves to notice the positives in our day that would otherwise slip away unnoticed. When we recognize our minds getting caught in the trap of negativity, we can use this as a cue to ask ourselves what we might be overlooking, and train ourselves to become detectives of positivity. Author Katrina Kenison, in her book *The Gift of an Ordinary Day,* writes poignantly about how being present to the ordinary, even seemingly mundane moments of everyday life can transform the unremarkable into something extraordinary (Kenison, 2009). Here is an example of that:

About five or six years ago, I was driving to Burlington, Vermont, when I stopped in Dartmouth, New Hampshire, to eat lunch along the way. Sitting in a local restaurant, I noticed a man situated at a nearby table with his daughter, who looked about five-years old. This was an ordinary lunch, nothing more. However, something struck me about this pair and I couldn't help but watch them. In fact, I was so captivated that I still remember this in detail and enjoy retelling the story, even though it occurred many years ago. Often, when parents sit with their young children, they are somewhat attentive, but not fully present. They might be checking their cell phone periodically, or half listening to their child as they also think about other things.

What was so striking to me in watching this father was that he was completely attentive to every word his daughter said. He made full eye contact, leaned in, responded thoughtfully to each remark. He had the body language of someone who was fully engaged. It was as if every word and gesture of hers mattered more than anything else. What could have been just an ordinary lunch turned into a profound opportunity for connection and presence. I remember thinking to myself how lucky this little girl was to have someone so present and attentive in her life, and how lucky for this man not to miss this chance to create something extraordinary out of an otherwise routine lunch. What if we lived even a few moments of every day like that? Such is the power of the magnifying glass.

As another example, I recall one evening feeling particularly irritable after a long day. I was tired and had just left the grocery store to head home. My mind was caught up in thoughts of how much I still had to do, and how I probably wasn't going to get it all done. This increased the irritability I was already feeling. Thankfully, in this moment I remembered to use my tools (as I *try* to do). I looked up and noticed the most spectacular sky, turning pink and golden as the sun was setting through the clouds. I paused and took in this magnificent sunset, which I almost entirely missed by being caught up in the negative thoughts in my head. Noticing this sunset, and magnifying the accompanying feelings of awe, helped to shift my outlook and mood. I recognized this experience of the sunset as a passing moment of time on this planet, in this solar system. I felt uplifted, and showed up for the rest of the evening very differently.

Ava and her husband Tom sought parental guidance because their two young boys, ages five and seven, were misbehaving regularly. The children were frequently oppositional and even defiant, and Ava and Tom were caught in a negative feedback loop where they would yell at the boys for their misbehavior, and then the boys would feel badly and see themselves as "bad kids," and act accordingly.

What Ava and Tom realized as they began to pay attention to their own behavior, was that they frequently missed the small, positive moments when the boys were behaving appropriately, being helpful, or listening, because these moments were overpowered by the negative ones, which in their minds, demanded the most attention. When they began carrying the magnifying glass into their day, they started to see the moments of good behavior throughout the day that they had otherwise missed. They began to catch the positive behavior and reward it with immediate praise and appreciation. In addition, they made a point of setting aside "special time" with each child, one-on-one, when they would get on the floor and play something of their son's choosing, while being fully engaged in this quality time together. These small, consistent changes in their own behavior made a huge difference in decreasing their sons' misbehavior and creating a more positive family environment for all.

Dean struggled with feelings of insecurity and a sense that he wasn't good enough, despite outside circumstances that told a different story; he was highly successful at his job, well liked, and had many friends. It was easy for Dean to notice all the things that he believed were "wrong" with him, and all of the moments when he wished he handled things differently, did a better job, or sounded "smarter." When Dean began carrying the magnifying glass with him, he was surprised to discover many positive qualities about himself and moments in his day when he felt competent; moments he easily overlooked much of the time.

On a given day, some of the things Dean noticed and focused on were: calling his parents and recognizing himself as a caring and loving son; assisting coworkers solve a challenging problem and appreciating his competency for analytical thinking and troubleshooting; helping his friend with a relationship difficulty and seeing himself as a compassionate and devoted friend. With each of these situations, Dean allowed himself to acknowledge and appreciate the beneficial qualities he noticed, while focusing on taking in the positive, accompanying emotions. After several weeks doing this, he began to feel empowered and to view himself in a different manner, recognizing himself as a person with a lot to offer.

~ Look around carefully. In any given moment, there are hundreds if not thousands of places you could rest your attention. Where are you choosing to rest your attention right now?

~ See if you notice one positive moment about your day right now. You might think about something significant in your life that you are grateful for, such as a loved one, but you might also notice something smaller, such as having this quiet moment to read and take care of yourself, or feeling the fresh air and gentle breeze as it blows throught the window.

~ Whatever you choose to focus on, spend at least thirty seconds savoring the experience and taking in a felt sense of it by feeling the positive emotions spreading throughout your body. Get curious about how positivity shows up in your body.

Strengthening the Velcro Muscle in a Helpful Way

I want to share a strategy I call "Retelling the Story" that can help strengthen our ability to use the magnifying glass within our day, even when at first it may feel too challenging to do so in the actual moment.

Retelling the Story

The exercise of "Retelling the Story" is a way of working with the magnifying glass by looking back on the day, seeing what was missed, and retelling the day's events from a different perspective. After the retelling, there is an opportunity to take in what is good and helpful about this new story or perspective. This is a way of training your mind to become more like Velcro for the positives in the day. With some practice, it then becomes easier to go through your day and catch these positive moments as they arise.

Morgan (from Chapter One) ran a big corporation and struggled with a Velcro problem in which she tended to notice everything that wasn't going well, but had a harder time recognizing the positives among her employees. Although it was a strength to be able to hone in on problems and fix them, her approach was too one-sided and had a negative impact on morale at the office. Morgan began to make a point at the end of each day to write down everything she could remember about the day from a more positive perspective. She asked herself: "What went smoothly today? Who was exhibiting positive leadership qualities? What got accomplished that helped us move toward our goals? What employees displayed strengths of focus, effective communication, creativity or efficiency? What contributions did the team make as a whole toward our overall mission?"

She found that when she wrote these things down, she not only identified many more things than she would normally have noticed, but she also shifted her own mood to one of greater optimism and enthusiasm. She found this practice so helpful that she began to send around a daily email to her employees recapping the positives. This action made a noticeable difference, boosting morale and increasing motivation in the work environment.

Monique, from Chapter One, found herself caught up in frequent negativity that left her feeling depleted. In addition to the day-to-day challenges she faced, she was grappling with the realization that she did not have the ideal life she had envisioned for herself due to some poor choices she had made in recent years. As she focused on the negatives in her day and life, she found herself increasingly anxious and depressed. Monique found it hard to notice any positives in her day as it was unfolding, but she had an easier time "Retelling the Story" by looking back at the end of her day and noticing what she missed. Even though she often came home in a bad mood after work, when she went over her day she was able to magnify many positive moments she had overlooked. She wrote these down and spent a few minutes taking in the positive emotions of each thing she wrote down.

For example, on one particular day she wrote: "Even though traffic was bad this morning, I got to talk with a friend over the phone who I hadn't connected with in a long time; Yes, my stepson drives me crazy by leaving his stuff all over the house, but I really appreciated how he cleaned up the dishes in the sink without my needing to ask today; Despite the usual stressors at work, my presentation went really well and my ideas were well received and made a positive impact." By spending time doing this on a regular basis, Monique began to notice a shift in her mood and energy. Over time, she became more adept at using her magnifying glass throughout the day.

~ Go back over the events of your day today.

~ Retell the story and notice anything you may have missed. Take in any positive moments in your day by magnifying any feelings of appreciation, gratitude or joy, however large or small.

Magnifying the Silver Lining

We can use the magnifying glass during trying times to help us find meaning and purpose, even amidst serious challenges. When we magnify the silver lining, we don't overlook important things that need our attention, or push away difficult feelings that may be there (see the previous chapter), but we choose to focus on what is helpful and beneficial amidst our challenges.

One of my friends was at my house recently for an outdoor gathering. She walked around a side of our house where we don't often walk, and tripped in a hidden gopher hole, fracturing four of her toes! (As you might imagine, I felt terrible!) When I saw this friend the next week, she told me that she was grateful this had happened. She said she saw it as an opportunity for her to slow down and take some extra, needed time away from work. Her mother had recently died, and she had intended to return to work the day after the gathering at my house. Having injured her foot, she was forced to take off additional time at work. Taking some extra time allowed her to give herself the emotional space and attention she might not have otherwise received. Rather than focus on the fact that she was laid up, had to be in a boot for many weeks, and was inconvenienced in many regards (all of which were true), she chose to focus on something helpful and meaningful in the situation. While she didn't deny some of the more upsetting emotions about this situation, she truly embraced the time that she had to slow down and ease back into work.

Another one of my friends was diagnosed many years ago with lymphoma. (Thankfully she has since fully recovered and is healthy and doing well.) During the time that she was sick and undergoing treatment, she had an amazing attitude about her illness and healing. She saw her illness as an opportunity to slow down, wake up, and become more present in her life. Rather than focus completely on all the negative side effects of the medications and the aspects of her life she had to put on hold, she chose to magnify the moments in her day that brought her meaning and purpose. That didn't mean that she was not immensely affected by the enormity of this illness, or that she didn't feel frequent sadness, fear and anger. She allowed herself to feel these emotions. But she chose to magnify what was good in her day that she could have easily missed. She spent more time in nature and truly savored this time. She focused on taking care of herself, and appreciated a slower pace of life and more time for reflection.

Magnifying these positive moments in her life helped her face her health crisis with greater resilience, and even discover some hidden joys despite some extremely difficult circumstances.

~

~   Think of a difficulty you might be going through, large or small. Without ignoring anything important about the situation, or pushing aside any difficult feelings about it, see what you might magnify that could help you face the challenge in a beneficial way. Perhaps, for example, you might hover your magnifying glass over the people in your life who are supportive as you face this challenge. Take in their support, care and concern as a felt experience of positivity in your body.

Magnifying Using Our Imagination

Sometimes the things that we choose to magnify were right in front of us all along. However, there is also benefit to magnifying experiences that we call up in our minds that may not be occurring in this moment. During much of our lives, our imaginations can play out worst-case scenarios that contribute to our worries and fears. However, we can learn to use our imaginations to work in our favor and to be beneficial to us. Through our imaginations, we can evoke and call up positive emotional experiences that occurred in the past that we can then magnify and savor —such as remembering a time when we handled a challenging situation with competence or equanimity.

When we re-experience that sense of calmness or equanimity (or whatever it might be), it becomes a resource that we can then draw on in our current lives (Hanson, 2014). We can even call up positive emotional experiences that may never have occurred, as long as we can vividly imagine these moments. For example, I could imagine myself on a beautiful beach in the Caribbean where I have never actually been. As I experience the calmness and serenity of this imagined place, those feelings become resources available to me in *this* moment that I can access and carry into my day.

Once Dean (from the example above) was comfortable carrying the magnifying glass with him, he began to also use it to recall past times in his life when he felt competent, to remind himself of the qualities already within him that were available to access. For example, when he found himself feeling insecure about an upcoming social situation, he recalled multiple times when he handled himself well at big work galas where he had to interact with people he never met before. When he found himself feeling insecure at work, he recalled recent reviews when he was told how much his skills were an asset to his company. As he recalled each of these experiences, he took in the accompanying, positive feelings associated with them, and he magnified these feelings so that they were very vivid. He remembered what it was like to feel confident and competent, and as he embodied that feeling it gave him positive energy to carry into his current, unfolding day.

Jing worked in an environment in which she was surrounded by negativity. As much as she liked her coworkers, there was a lot of gossip and complaining among them. She often felt caught in the middle of it, even though it didn't involve her personally. It was easy for her to take in other people's negativity, and when she did so, she experienced a great deal of stress that drained her energy. In order to prevent this from happening, Jing began to take three to five-minute breaks at work, in which she would imagine herself in a safe, secluded, favorite beach spot. As she imagined being there, she experienced a deep sense of peace and relaxation that she was able to magnify and savor. Doing this was like giving herself a mini-vacation, and she found that she was able to return to her work with greater energy, a feeling of being replenished, and a greater ability to prevent the surrounding negativity from swallowing her up.

~

Dialing In What You Might Need

~ As you go through your day, think about what you most need today. Do you need compassion, relaxation, courage, serenity or perhaps something else? Whatever it might be, see if you can call that feeling up in your mind by thinking about a time when you felt that way, and re-experience it now.

~ Recall as much detail as possible about the past situation so that it becomes vivid in your mind and body. As you do so, magnify whatever positive emotions or sensations you notice in your body, and rest there for a few minutes. What benefits do you notice in doing this?

Additional Practice

Growing Your Skills

In the weeks to come, practice developing your magnifying glass skills. See each day as an opportunity to practice at least one or more of the previous exercises. To do this, write down the following on a notecard and carry it with you as a reminder. (Make sure to look at it often.)

> Magnify what is in front of me
> Retell the story
> Magnify the silver lining
> Magnify using my imagination

Look for opportunities to do these exercises throughout your day. It need not take much time. Even just a minute or two—if done with awareness and presence—can be beneficial.

At the end of each day, write down at least one thing that you experienced in your day using the magnifying glass. As you write it down, take a moment to take in and acknowledge the felt sense of positivity in your body.

Beginning Your Day with the Magnifying Glass

Make it a point to begin your day by using the magnifying glass within the first few minutes of waking up. Notice something positive that you might otherwise overlook. It might be as simple as taking an extra thirty seconds to look out the window and notice the sunlight shining through the leaves of the trees; giving a family member an extra long hug,—or feeling your breath and thinking about how amazing it is that your heart has been pumping steadily and continuously since the moment you were born.

Sharing the Magnifying Glass with Others

This activity can be done in the workplace or at home.

Take a small jar or container and place it in a central location. Every day invite each household member or a co-worker to write something positive on a slip of paper and put it into the jar. It could be something you notice about another person (e.g., I was grateful for Barbara's help today with the new computer program; Jeremy showed great courage jumping into the deep end of the swimming pool even though he was scared), or something positive about your own experience (I got a lot accomplished on my project today; I enjoyed having time to garden before work this morning; I'm so grateful that my mother's doctor appointment went well today).

At the end of the week, take turns reading what was written on each slip of paper and savoring the positivity.

CHAPTER SIX

The Beacon: Finding Meaning and Purpose in an Uncertain World

I REMEMBER THE DAY VIVIDLY. It was a Sunday in June, but it felt like a cold March day. The temperature was only in the low 50s and the wind and driving rain made it feel much colder. The day before, I had biked seventy-five miles as part one of a two-day charity ride to raise money for multiple sclerosis, the first long bike ride of this sort that I had ever done. Sunday was part two and the weather was about as bad as one could imagine for a June day. I had seventy-five miles in front of me to complete, and I was almost immediately soaked through and through. I knew I had to stop for some food and drink at the rest stops along the way so as not to run out of "fuel," but the difficulty of keeping my body warm from the driving rain, wind, and cold made it nearly impossible to stop for more than a few minutes without shivering uncontrollably. As much as it was a physical challenge to complete this second seventy-five-mile ride, it was equally a mental challenge.

What I remember about that day was that there were three things that helped me most:

1. I kept my focus on the "finish line"—on why it mattered so much to me to complete this ride. I thought about all the people who struggle

with multiple sclerosis and the commitment I had made to raise money to help researchers find a cure or better treatments. I also thought about my personal goal of achieving something for which I had trained hard and never imagined being able to do.

2. I broke the ride down into small increments in my mind. I didn't think about having to ride seventy-five miles, much less in these terrible weather conditions. That would have been completely overwhelming. I thought about doing a ten-mile ride to the next rest stop. I could do ten miles—that's only two laps around the lake where I often bike: not a big deal, I thought to myself. I was present for those ten miles and nothing more. When I completed the first ten miles, I focused on the next ten, and so on. (Singing out loud helped too. Thank goodness no one was close enough to hear me!)

3. I had practiced riding regularly. Biking had become part of my weekly routine. It wasn't like I just showed up and expected to ride 150 miles in two days. I had already been doing it, little by little, week by week, with my training rides of thirty miles here, forty miles there, etc. The individual pieces were familiar to me. I just needed to string them together in somewhat new circumstances.

Tool Five: The Beacon

How do we live a meaningful life? Perhaps that is a million-dollar question, but I think it is one that is critical to ask. More specifically, how can we identify what is most important to us, what we most value, who we most want to be—and then align our actions with those values and the vision of our best self, so that we can show up each day from this place? There are plenty of people who look back on their lives with deathbed regrets, wishing they had lived differently. We don't have to wait until we get to that point.

We live in uncertain times, in an uncertain world. There is much that we can't control in our lives and in our world. Sometimes, we are thrown curve balls that we don't expect. But there is one thing of which we can be certain; we can control our own behavior and our own daily choices. And if these choices align with what we most value and who we want to be, then we open up to the richness of our lives, no matter our circumstances.

Actually, there is one other thing we can be certain of—and that is uncertainty.

Uncertainty and change are a natural part of life, and something that we all face on a regular basis. There are no guarantees. And even though we may cling to things as they are now, change is inevitable. So how do we pursue what matters most to us when things are always changing, and when we can't always know the outcome or whether things will go as expected? An important part of moving toward our goals is accepting uncertainty, change, vulnerability, and the discomfort that goes with it, as natural parts of our experience. Rather than letting the discomfort stop us from going after what we want, or thinking we need to get rid of it, we can learn to bring it along with us for the ride in order to live the life that we want. This important teaching—a basic premise of Acceptance and Commitment Therapy (Hayes, 2005)—offers valuable wisdom for living a meaningful life.

> *A beacon is a light or signal that is in a prominent place, that serves as a guide for airplanes or ships at sea, and helps them find their way. The Beacon is a tool that allows us to hold a larger vision of what is most important and who we most want to be, out in front of us as motivation to become our best selves each day.*

Use of the beacon involves identifying what we most value and then aligning our actions to match this best version of ourselves. It is about holding out intentions for ourselves, developed from a place of wisdom and knowing what it best for us, and making choices to reach those intended goals by challenging ourselves each day to take small, measurable steps that add up over time. It isn't about being overly focused on the absolute outcome or end point, but it is about taking inspired actions to find value in the daily Finish Line, the small steps each day that can make today's journey more meaningful.

Don't be misled by the wording here and get hung up on trying to achieve goals, such as wanting to have $1,000 by next week or needing to be promoted by next month. There is nothing wrong with having those kinds of goals but what I am talking about here has more to do with the values behind those goals: for example, taking daily steps to become financially independent, or taking daily actions to show effective leadership skills at work that earn the respect of others. The beacon is not so much about focusing on a specific outcome, as on understanding why that outcome is important to us. When we can hold the beacon in the distance but within sight each day, it reminds us how we want to show up today and it motivates us and keeps us aligned with that vision.

Sometimes while driving, I have encountered flashing signs on the side of the road displaying the speed of my car, along with an indication of the speed I am *supposed* to be driving. When I see those two numbers, it is a good reminder for me to make sure I adjust my speed to match the designated speed limit. The beacon works in a similar way. Holding out a vision of who I want to be today helps motivate me to adjust my behavior to match that vision.

What Stops Us from Being Our Best Selves?

We are human. We are imperfect. We often have all kinds of visions for ourselves, but it is easy to fall short of these visions, or to abandon them altogether. We might want to be more patient; to overcome our fears and do something new; to take better care of our health by exercising regularly or eating healthier; to spend more quality time with those we love and less time on electronics or work; to make more time for ourselves; to embark on a creative endeavor; or to give up an unhealthy habit. If change were easy, we wouldn't have so many self-help books (I'd be out of luck) or diet books. Even when we know intellectually what is best for us, it is often hard to follow through.

As health psychologist Kelly McGonigal explains so beautifully (McGonigal, 2017), it is often as if we have competing parts of ourselves; the wise part, that knows what would be best for us in the grand scheme, and the impulsive part, that wants immediate gratification and wants to feel good in the moment (even if that doesn't serve our best, long term interest). Dr. McGonigal explains the brain science behind this; there are actually competing parts of our brain circuitry that "feed" each of these "selves." When we do something that is uncomfortable (for example, pushing ourselves to exercise when we would rather hang on the couch, or raising our hand to contribute at work when it would be so much more comfortable to remain silent), one of the areas of our brain that is activated is the part that controls our fight-or-flight response. It can feel threatening to step out of our comfort zone, even when doing so can ultimately be good for us. In addition to that false alarm going off in these situations, the part of our brain that drives us to seek pleasure and avoid discomfort can make it a lot easier for us to stay with our same old behavior because who wants to be uncomfortable anyway? (Here's where the tool "the door" can come in handy!)

It is easy to see how some of our other evolutionary challenges might play a role in stopping us from making positive change in our life. For example, we might be unaware that we aren't living our life as our best self if we are caught in the day-to-day ruminations that take us away from living in the present moment. How often do we go through the motions of our day and not really stop and pay attention to these things? Did you wake up this morning and ask yourself, "Who do I most want to be today and what is most important to me about how I show up today?" I know I never used to ask myself those questions. Our negative self-talk and the noisy person at the movie theater who rents space in our head can also prevent us from making changes, by keeping us trapped in self-doubt, fears of failure and unworthiness, and language that convinces us that "I can't" and "I won't ever" are absolute truths. In addition, the Velcro problem and our tendency to get caught up in negativity can take up a lot of energy in our lives and not create a conducive environment for change.

The beacon is a helpful tool that can be used in combination with any of the other tools in this book to help you address these evolutionary challenges by providing motivation to make optimal choices in the face of a pull to do otherwise.

There are three common roadblocks we may encounter on our journey toward taking meaningful action in our lives:

1. When we know something is good for our well-being but we aren't doing it (e.g., exercising, getting to bed early, setting aside a few minutes during the day to replenish);

2. When we engage in behaviors that we know aren't good for us or don't align with who we want to be, but we do them anyway (e.g., yelling frequently at our kids, engaging in unhealthy habits, snapping at coworkers, overworking ourselves); and

3. When we don't notice our behavior in the first place and plow along without being tuned in to what is important to us.

By using the beacon as a tool to guide us, we can make healthier choices by engaging the higher thinking parts of our brain rather than acting from our more primitive brain and/or habitual patterns. When we ask ourselves, "Why does this matter?" or "Why is this important to me," we access a bigger picture that can help us see long term benefits for our future self. When we focus on the value and importance of what matters most, it also becomes easier to tolerate discomfort because we are on a path to something greater, and thus are more willing to take actions that align with our best self (McGonigal, 2017). And when we take the time to ask the big questions in the first place, we allow ourselves to notice behaviors we may not otherwise pay attention to at all.

~   Take a moment and identify what behaviors in your life you would like to be doing but aren't.

~   Now name some behaviors you would like to stop doing but haven't been able to.

~   Finally, identify the behaviors that you engage in on a regular basis that align well with who you are and who you want to be. Make sure to spend some time with this one, as there may be many more behaviors than you initially realized. Ask yourself what helps you make these helpful choices on a consistent basis in your life?

Using the Beacon to Show Up as Our Best Selves

It is helpful to keep in mind a few guiding principles when using the beacon as a tool.

1. Spend some time identifying what is important to you in various aspects of your life (for example work, family, friendships, personal time), and what qualities you most value about the person you are and the person you want to be. You can do this in a deeper way by meditating, journaling, or discussing these answers with a partner or friend. However, you can also do this on a daily basis in a brief way by asking yourself, "How do I want to show up as my best self today?" and envisioning what this might look like, even before you get out of bed each day.

2. When possible, if you are trying to make changes in your behavior and your daily actions, break things down into smaller, manageable, concrete steps. If eating healthier is important to you because you want to have more energy and vitality, think about small actions you can take today that will align with your vision of who you want to be. Rather than focusing on "needing to lose fifty pounds," focus on your beacon (creating greater health and vitality) and choose a small step to take today that will lead you in this direction (perhaps making healthy choices today by substituting water for soda and juices.)

3. String together these small steps with consistency and repetition. See each day as an opportunity to practice, and build in the understanding that you are human and will slip back into old patterns at times even as you move toward that

beacon. Keep your eye on the beacon and be gentle with yourself as you welcome each day as a new opportunity to align your actions with who you most want to be.

4. Have a plan for handling setbacks. As Dr. Robert Brooks explains, a cornerstone of a resilient mindset involves being able to deal with setbacks (Brooks & Goldstein, 2001). Remember that a ship may be blown off course at times, but if it keeps the beacon in sight it will eventually find its way to port. That ship that blows off course doesn't just resign itself to forever being adrift at sea. It keeps looking for the beacon and making adjustments in its course to get back on track.

The following are examples of how the beacon can be used as a tool to help address each of the five evolutionary challenges that we have been exploring.

Using the Beacon to Help with the False Alarm

Jane struggled with anxiety from a young age and found over the years that some of the things she most wanted to do triggered her fight-or-flight response in a way that challenged her. She experienced intense anxiety in her body when she wanted to join the school play, when she was asked on a date, when she had to drive on the highway, when she had to speak in front of others, and when she was on a plane. Her first inclination was to play it "safe" by avoiding these situations so as not to risk feeling the anxiety in her body. However, doing so made her world smaller and smaller as she cut herself off from the experiences that mattered most to her.

The beacon was a helpful tool for Jane. She realized that she didn't have to make her anxiety go away and put off the things she wanted to do until that day when her anxiety disappeared (which, she realized, might never happen). Instead, she practiced taking her anxiety with her (picturing it metaphorically "in the back seat," instead of the driver's seat) while holding out a vision of what was most important to her and why. She loved the camaraderie of being in the school play and feeling part of something collaborative and larger than herself. Driving on the highway saved her a tremendous amount of time and allowed her to visit friends who would otherwise be inaccessible. Flying on an airplane enabled her to travel to parts of the country that she found fascinating and exciting.

Jane began to break things down into little steps for herself, in order to create small successes that added up over time. For example, at first she drove to only one exit on the highway; she practiced a monologue in front of her sisters, and then her parents, and then her aunts and uncles; she went on several double dates before venturing on a date by herself. By focusing on the beacon and taking small but consistent steps toward it, she was able to engage in actions she might otherwise have avoided, in order to live the life she most wanted.

Using the Beacon to Stay Present and Engaged (and Switch out of Mind-Wandering)

Matias worked full time and had two young children at home, ages two and four. At the end of a long day and on weekends, he had fallen into the habit of spending long periods of time surfing the web, checking his phone, and using electronics to provide a kind of mindless distraction to numb out. This behavior became quite automatic, and it was hard for him to stop. However, when he focused on his beacon and asked himself what was most important to him in his role as a father, he remembered his own childhood and how his father rarely spent time with him. His grandfather, in contrast, would get down on the floor to play and showed interest in the things he enjoyed. It was important to Matias to be an engaged father, because he knew how it felt to have an unengaged one. He knew how vital it was for him as a young boy to feel seen and heard and validated by an adult in his life—his grandfather. Having an adult notice him in this way made a huge difference to him as he was growing up.

Matias began asking himself, "Who do I want to be when I walk in that door of my house?" and "How can I translate that into small, concrete actions today?" He decided that he would turn off his cell phone every evening when he walked in the door, and set aside fifteen minutes to play on the floor with his children. When he started to feel anxious that he should be checking his phone, he reminded himself of the value of being present in *this* moment with his kids.

Using the Beacon to Take the Noisy Person at the Movie Theater Lightly

Marnie was a smart and capable young woman, who doubted her own abilities. She often let the noisy person at the movie theater convince her that she wasn't good enough, especially in school, where she struggled due to a learning disability. It was easier for Marnie to give in to this voice and underachieve by not putting in much effort, rather than take the risk of trying and, in her mind, possibly "failing." When Marnie began working with the beacon, she realized that what was most essential to her in school was being the kind of person who worked to her full potential. That was important to her because she knew adults close to her who gave up their dreams and lived unsatisfying lives because of it. Holding her beacon out as a vision for herself, she explored how she could be that person on a daily basis—what actions she could take that would align with this vision of herself as someone who worked to their full potential. She had clear goals for her future, and she knew she would not get there by giving up on herself. She decided to set aside two hours every night to study in the college library away from distractions, and she set up an appointment with the college tutoring center to get help with some of her harder classes on a weekly basis. When she felt the inclination to give up and blow off her studying (when that internal self-critical voice became loud and dominating), she pictured her beacon and recalled how empowered she felt on days when she followed through with what she set out to do.

Using the Beacon to Help Tolerate Emotional Discomfort and Stay Aligned

Losing my mother at a young age left certain emotional imprints on me that became heightened when I became a mother. As I mentioned previously, one of the fears that I carried with me was the fear of loss, of losing those I love most deeply. While this fear is natural for many mothers, having experienced such a traumatic loss made it more difficult for me to gain distance from this emotion, and it led me to want to put my children in an imagined protective bubble where no harm could come to them. At different developmental stages, I found it challenging to "let them go" out into the world. When they were very young, I grew anxious about allowing them to go on long car rides with other families when I was not in control as the driver. When they started to drive, it was scary for me to let them get behind the wheel on their own. When they wanted to go abroad, this challenged me to my core. At each of these points when I felt the fear of letting my kids go out on their own, it was helpful for me to hold a beacon out for myself, to remind myself that I wanted to be a mother who encouraged her children to grow their own wings and explore the world with curiosity, excitement and a sense of confidence. Holding them back to give myself some illusionary feeling of safety was not in their best interest, and not who I wanted to be. Being able to focus on this beacon helped me to tolerate my own anxieties and fears and align my actions with this best vision of myself.

Using the Beacon to Rise Above Negativity

Tracie and John had been married for ten years and had two young children. Their marriage was not going well, and it impacted all of them. John had a tendency to criticize Tracie over petty things and make frequent negative remarks, something he had learned from watching his own father's behavior toward his mother. Tracie was hurt by John's criticism and felt that he was disrespectful to her at these times. Because this pattern had been going on for some time, Tracie began to pull away in the relationship and took less interest in spending time with John. This made John feel disconnected from the person he cared most about, and at the same time angry at her lack of interest and attention.

The situation came to a head when their older son's second grade teacher reported that their son was being mean and disrespectful toward the other children. John became concerned that he was not being a good role model, and that his son might be modeling his behavior. In addition, neither he nor Tracie was happy in the relationship, as neither of their needs were being met. John began to ask himself who he wanted to be in this marriage and realized that he was falling short of his vision and the person he knew he was capable of being. He also knew that he wanted to be a positive role model for his children. To remind him of what was important to him, he placed a photo next to his bed of him and his wife when they first met, and a second photo of him holding his two children. He made a point of looking at the photos when he got out of bed each morning. This helped remind him of who he wanted to be for his children, and how loving, kind and attentive he acted when he first met his wife. John used this as a beacon and tried to hold it in his mind when he walked in the door at the end of the day. He became more aware of when he complained or criticized his wife. He caught himself at these times and made an effort to express more appreciation to her for the things she did. These efforts made Tracie want to spend more time with him and they became mutually reinforcing for both of them.

Using the Beacon to Open to Life's Possibilities

When we learn to use the beacon to hold out a vision of what is most important and meaningful to us without becoming attached to any particular outcome, without the end point defined in a particular way, we open up to all of life's possibilities and unfolding adventures. Some of the greatest scientific achievements and artistic contributions have occurred because their creators were not attached to a particular outcome. There is a quality we can cultivate of being guided and open to what arises, to letting the path unfold before us, while holding out a vision of what is important to us. When we can hold lightly the outcome or need for it to look just so, we open up to greater possibilities, creativity, adventures and discovery.

Sometimes when we are too goal driven, we can become constricted, tightly wound, and hyper-focused. We can miss seeing things around us, or options and choices that might be available, because they don't fit into our absolute plan, schema, or expected outcome. When we can keep our eyes on the beacon, but open to the possibility of multiple paths that might lead to where we want to go, we make room for surprise and delight, passion and playfulness that can add depth to our lives.

When my kids were babies, I left the psychology practice where I worked for the flexibility to be home with them full-time for a few years. I knew I wanted to do something professionally with all of my creative energy and channel it into something I was passionate about, but I didn't know what that was. I was someone who had planned out much of my life, so having this kind of open space and uncertainty felt strange to me. One day, I wandered into a small bookstore that I had heard good things about but had never visited before. I hadn't known exactly where it was located, but I happened to drive by it, and on a whim, I went inside. On the wall was a sign for a YogaKids™ training in Boston that caught my eye. I had never considered becoming a yoga teacher for children, but given that I greatly enjoyed my own yoga practice and loved working with children, this intrigued me. I ended up doing a year-long training, mostly from home, part-time and on my own schedule, and I loved it. This led me to teach classes in the community and the school, and was a step on my journey of teaching mind-body practices for health and wholeness. I had never imagined doing this or seeking out this field, but being able to stay in touch with my beacon while loosening some of my rigid expectations allowed me to discover something that was very fulfilling for me.

An Important Reminder

As I mentioned previously, it might be helpful to remind yourself on a regular basis that ships may be blown off course at times, but keeping the beacon in sight helps them to eventually find their way back home. Part of being human means that we make mistakes—a lot! Our imperfections lead us away from who we want to be, and what we set out to do, again and again. This is not a sign of weakness or failure, but rather a part of this common humanity we share. Change is often nonlinear. We slip, we fall, we take steps backwards, and then we pick ourselves up, brush ourselves off, reassess, and take wise actions in the direction we want to go. If we allow the voice of self-criticism or self-defeat to take over, we may stay stuck, or even sabotage ourselves. Cultivating the voice of self-compassion (see Chapter Three), and holding the beacon within sight, can help us work through obstacles and continue to move forward towards our goals with greater meaning and purpose.

For Your Practice

Personal Reflection for Developing Your Beacon

~ Identify what is most important to you in your personal and/ or work life. What qualities do you value in yourself? Who do you most want to be when you show up in your day?

~ If you were to translate that into concrete steps, things you could do today that would align with who you most want to be, what would those steps be? Be as specific as possible.

Using this formula can be helpful:

When I encounter X in my life today, I will respond by doing Y. For example, if you want to be more present as a parent in your child's life, you might say, "When my children come home from school today, I will set aside ten minutes of undivided attention to listen to whatever they would like to share." If you want to make more time for your personal well-being, you might say, "When my alarm (which I set ten minutes early) goes off today, I will sit outside and meditate or listen to the birds before getting ready for work." This suggestion comes from research on using "implementation intentions"—that is, visualizing in detail how you will reach a goal and linking anticipated situations with goal-directed actions (Gollwitzer & Sheeran, 2006)].

Anticipate any obstacles that might get in your way and plan what the wise self can say to your more impulsive self to help you align your actions with who you want to be. Focus on the beacon—why this goal is important to you.

Using the example above, "When my alarm goes off, I may want to hit the snooze button, but if that happens, I will remind myself that taking just a few minutes to recharge at the beginning of the day will help me create the kind of day that I want."

Beginning Your Day with Your Beacon

Before you get out of bed in the morning, simply ask yourself "who would I be today if I was living as my best self?"

Spend a few minutes visualizing going through your day as your best self. Not only think about what this would look like, but also picture it in your mind and feel how it might feel in your body to live as the fullest expression of yourself today.

Note that this exercise works especially well after completing the Personal Reflection for Developing Your Beacon on the previous page.

CHAPTER SEVEN

The Beginning: Coming Home to Our Own Open Hearts

W HEN I WAS QUITE YOUNG, I recall my father sharing his interest in spiders and spider webs. He told me spiders were amazing creatures and explained that the silk they created was the strongest possible material that could be used to make a web. He explained that even if humans tried, we would not be able to create a stronger, lighter material than the silk produced by spiders. He often pointed out spider webs when he saw them and marveled at their magnificence. I also recall as a young child that when there were thunder and lightning storms, my father would tell me that by listening and counting the seconds between the lightning and the sound of thunder, I could calculate how far away the storm was. I grew up quite fond of spiders (and I still am to this day), and not particularly fearful of thunderstorms.

Just down the road at my neighbor's house, my friend's mother was terrified of spiders. Whenever she saw one, she shrieked and carried on, often backing away from it in terror, or stomping on it when she got up the courage to do so. She also was anxious and upset whenever there were thunder and lightning storms and warned her children to stay away from windows and be vigilant if a storm was ever approaching. To this day, my friend is terrified of spiders and thunderstorms. Whenever she is confronted by either, her heart races and she feels anxious and uneasy.

Our Conditioning and Old Programs

We are not only influenced by the ancient neural programs that we inherited from our ancestors millions of years ago. We also are very much influenced by the early conditioning we experienced as young children, and the beliefs that we internalized about the world and ourselves at a young age. This conditioning, as I have seen time and again, can often be rewired, but it takes awareness, willingness, practice, skill, and patience to do so. The tools described in this book can help you rewire these old programs, whatever they may be (though keep in mind that, especially with severe adverse circumstances and traumatic situations, it might be important to work with a skilled therapist).

I was fortunate to grow up in a home with two loving parents, but my mother's sudden and tragic death when I was a teenager shattered my world. I no longer felt safe in the way I had and I carried an unease that at any minute something bad could happen to the people I loved most. This experience of traumatic loss tremendously heightened whatever anxiety may have been there already. It made it much easier for me to be triggered and sent into fight-or- flight when I faced even small, minor situations in which I felt I had little control. I have had to work hard to recognize this about myself and to continually use tools and strategies to help me overcome some of my initial reactions to these kinds of situations. Sometimes, I simply have to observe my reactions and recognize "This is coming from an old place." For example, there are times when I might worry or become anxious about something that I know is irrational, but I continue to feel that anxiety anyway. By being able to name it, sit with it compassionately, and observe it, I can avoid being swallowed up by it and work through it with greater ease.

For some of my patients, different kinds of early experiences have greatly impacted them. Some have grown up in physically or emotionally abusive homes and internalized harsh messages from their parents about not being good enough. Others have grown up in chaotic environments with well-meaning parents who had their own shortcomings and could not provide the emotional stability that would have been most helpful. But we need not experience "big" traumas to be impacted. Often, we learn to construct beliefs about ourselves and the world from the smaller, day-to-day difficulties and challenges that we experience growing up—for example, being called mean names at school, having a pet die, having our feelings hurt by a friend, being yelled at or misunderstood. Even well-meaning parents (myself included) say things out of anger or fear to our children that can sometimes become internalized in ways we never intended. In addition, the cultural expectations that we grow up with, and the media messages we are bombarded by play a significant role in the narratives that we tell ourselves early on.

We all desire to be loved, cherished, attended to, seen and heard as children. When we perceive that we are not, when the adults around us miss the mark in some way, as they often do, we tend to internalize this at a young age as proof that there is something lacking in us, that we are not good enough. This often happens even in nurturing environments with loving parents, just by nature of our limited ability when young to fully understand the world around us. In my family, my sister was born four years after me. Even though my parents loved us all very much (I have a brother two years older), I interpreted the new baby suddenly getting all of this attention as me not being enough in some way (or why else would my parents have had to have another child?). This belief that I was not enough was something I internalized and carried with me for a good part of my life, well into adulthood. I frequently meet and hear about successful and well-respected people who continually struggle with questions about their own worthiness. This is a more common occurrence than one may realize.

Unconsciously, we believe that these messages about our lack of worth are truth—and over time we may even create self-fulfilling prophesies based on these early, and often limited and inaccurate beliefs. The stories that we tell ourselves and the beliefs we hold can shape how we view the world, and influence what we see. Remember that at any given moment, there are hundreds or thousands of things that we might focus our attention on. If a person believes "I'm not good enough," he/she may unconsciously look for things in the environment to support that world view, even if there are many more aspects of their immediate world that refute this view. We often choose to interpret the world in a way that fits with our early stories.

Consider the example of Donna. While her parents loved her very much, they needed to give more time and attention to her younger sister, who had a significant and chronic medical condition. Donna grew up misunderstanding her parents' behavior. She believed that she wasn't enough, that she was less important and "invisible." Later, as a young adult, when people came into a room and didn't come right over to her, she interpreted this as proof that people didn't care about her. She would do little to initiate conversations, and others interpreted her quiet, withdrawn behavior as a signal that she wanted to be left alone. This behavior then reinforced her world view, and her early belief became a self-fulfilling prophesy for her. Even when people did show an interest in initiating conversations with her, she dismissed this as irrelevant because it didn't fit into her original scheme of being "invisible" and unimportant. Donna didn't even realize she was doing this. Only once she gained awareness of these old, habitual patterns could she loosen the grasp they had on her.

It can be very helpful to recognize how human we all are, and how common are our struggles! To know that we are far from perfect, that there is no such thing as an ideal relationship, that marriages are fraught with challenges, parent-child relationships try us to our core, self-doubt eats away at us even in the face of great success, greed and jealousy visit even the most compassionate people, fears keep us all awake at times, and even the most put-together people have meltdowns and breakdowns; this can be refreshing and relieving to know. Some of the most helpful presentations I have heard by other psychologists have been the ones in which the speakers reveal how very human they are. Suddenly, I don't feel so alone.

Personal and spiritual growth depend on us being able to embrace our own "muck"—not only the things we like about ourselves, but the parts that we dislike, or that make us uncomfortable. Rather than pushing away or disowning these parts of ourselves, coming home to ourselves means acknowledging the whole of who we are. This doesn't mean we have to accept our "bad behavior" (I can acknowledge my jealousies or insecurities while learning to not act on them in hurtful ways); but it does mean accepting the parts of ourselves that we would prefer to hide from the public eye, and perhaps even from our own view.

I believe that when we come into the world, we manifest the essence of who we are, and we are whole. Some spiritual teachers refer to this as our "true nature." Watch a very young child or even a baby and you might discover what I mean. There is often a natural sense of wonder, movement, curiosity, discovery, presence, play, creativity, laughter, and joy. This often gets lost along the way as we experience minor or major hurts—and as the invisible walls come down to protect us. The messages that we internalize about who we should be, what we need to do to be loved or get approval, what parts of ourselves we need to put away because they are unacceptable to others, often cause us to contract, constrict, conform, close off parts of ourselves, feel less than or unworthy and move away from a sense of wholeness and aliveness.

Returning to our true nature, and coming home to our own open hearts, requires an awakening. It requires us to be aware enough of the automatic programs that we are operating from to be able to see new possibilities. It means waking up to what we are sensing in our bodies (since we often cut ourselves off from this information), to what we are feeling (we often don't pay attention), to what we are thinking (which as we saw earlier can affect us more than we realize), and to how we are acting (in order to recognize what is and isn't working and make more conscious and intentional choices).

The tools in this book can help you do this. Coming home means establishing a felt sense of safety and an anchor of stability within; an ability to see things from a larger perspective; a way to experience presence, and self-compassion; the ability to accept things as they unfold in this moment; to trust in your own resources to be with whatever is here; and to appreciate your own strengths and the gifts available to you each day that can allow for greater joy. It is about experiencing ourselves as whole even with all of our imperfections. Being imperfect does not mean we are defective, broken, unworthy or less than—it simply means that we are human; imperfect, but whole. Perhaps what personal and spiritual growth truly involves is not so much an awakening as a *reawakening*, because it is about coming back to who we really are, at our core. To reawaken, we must be able to recognize the old programs that we are operating under and become unhooked from them.

How to Unhook from Our Old Programs

All of the tools in this book can help you to recognize which patterns, habits and behaviors are old and no longer serve you, and how you can step out of these old patterns and have greater choice in your life. Sometimes that choice might just be recognizing that you are being pulled into an old, unhelpful pattern. That observation may create the space to respond more wisely.

1. When you shine the flashlight of awareness, you may notice ways that you are reacting to old conditioning and evolutionary wiring that may not serve you anymore. The flashlight can help you bring the focus of your attention to the present moment to help you step out of past scripts and create new ones, based on today's realities.

2. The diet can help you see how old beliefs and thoughts may be keeping you trapped. It can help you realize that you are not your thoughts, and this can help free you from this self-imposed prison in your mind.

3. The door can help you sit with some of the younger hurt or scared parts of yourself in a compassionate way; to soothe and

attend to these parts, rather than push them away.

4. The magnifying glass can help you see things you might not have noticed and develop new schemas for experiencing the world (e.g., noticing the ways that you are worthy, loving, and loved).

5. Finally, keeping your eye on the beacon of light can help you to approach what is most important to you, even if there is some discomfort or vulnerability in doing so (that may stem from early experiences and beliefs).

When used all together, these tools can offer you a way to break free from old programs and patterns that may be keeping you stuck. An important point to emphasize here is that breaking free from old patterns does not necessarily mean that they disappear forever, never to rear their ugly heads. We may continue to have emotions or thoughts that are part of these old programs. But the difference is that once we have tools to recognize and work with what is arising, we can RESPOND differently to what is there; it no longer needs to have such a hold on us.

When I run into situations where something arises that I can't control, it no longer sends me into that place of intense and overwhelming panic and fear that it once did. Those fears and anxieties are still there and I feel them, but I can meet these emotions with a greater awareness, understanding, and a sense of compassion that allows me to experience more ease in moving through whatever is occurring. And sometimes, the things that used to feel like an "8" on my 1–10 meter now only register as a "3."

Each of the evolutionary challenges that we discussed in Chapter One may also intermix with early childhood challenges. For example, for some people, early traumas may make that alarm bell sound especially loud and continuously throughout their life, even long after the trauma has ended. If one internalizes the critical voice of a parent from childhood, the noisy person at the movie theater may sound a lot like that critical parent. We all have a tendency to see the world through a negative bias, but if a child grew up with adversity, that Velcro may be particularly sticky.

You may recall from Chapter One that when we work with challenge number one, the false alarm, we can establish a felt **sense of safety and stability within.**

When we work with challenge number two, the dial stuck in an unhelpful place, we can develop **presence, coming back to this moment.**

When we work with challenge number three, the noisy person at the movie theater, we can practice **self-compassion and perspective.**

When we work with challenge number four, the finger trap dilemma, we can grow **trust (that we can handle what is there) and acceptance.**

When we work with challenge number five, the Velcro problem, we can open the way for **gratitude and joy.**

When we recognize our old conditioning and work with the challenges it generates, we can develop an alternative to unhelpful or outdated old programs that we may have internalized and carried with us into adulthood. Thinking of this in another way, by working with the five challenges and using the tools laid out in this book, we can grow the inner resources of safety, presence, self-compassion, perspective, trust and acceptance, gratitude and joy.

~

~ What are some of your old, conditioned programs and beliefs that no longer serve you? Notice how these programs, beliefs and responses may have helped you when you were younger by trying to protect you in some way.

~ What do you miss in your life now when you continue to operate from these old, automatic programs?

An Exercise for Growing Inner Resources

As you go through your day, every time that you become aware of reacting out of old habits to a false alarm, or find your dial stuck in unhelpful mind-wandering, or hear the noisy person at the movie theater, or notice you are avoiding emotions calling your attention, or recognize your mind is being like Velcro for the negative —pause and think of this as an ***opportunity*** to practice growing and strengthening inner resources. Reframing your challenges for yourself in this way will allow you to move through them with greater ease and practice wiring in new responses. You can even think of each challenge as an opportunity to ***transform*** symptoms (see below) into lasting resources.

INSTRUCTIONS:

1. Use this guide below to help you notice challenges arising in your day.

2. Every time that you notice, know that you are stepping out of automatic pilot mode.

3. Ask yourself: Is this an old habit or program I am falling into? A habitual reaction that no longer serves me?

4. Remind yourself of the inner resources you are strengthening as you bring greater awareness to the experience at hand and respond more consciously. If it is helpful, copy this list below and carry it with you. Look for any ways to transform these obstacles into opportunities for growth.

False Alarm

- Symptoms:
  Anxiety, Fear and Stress

- Resources to Grow:
  Safety, Stability in the here and now

- Essential Tools:
  All, but especially Flashlight, Diet

Dial Stuck in an Unhelpful Place

- Symptoms:
  Distraction, Wandering Thoughts, Feelings of Dissatisfaction

- Resources to Grow:
  Presence (being in the moment) and Satisfaction/Authentic Happiness

- Essential Tools:
  All, but especially Flashlight

Noisy Person in the Movie Theater

- Symptoms:
  Distorted Thinking, Self-Criticism, Shame, Blame, Negative Ruminations

- Resources to Grow:
  Perspective, Self-Compassion

- Essential Tools:
  All, but especially Flashlight, Diet

Finger Trap Dilemma

- Symptoms:
  Avoidance, Numbing Out, Unease, Addictive Behaviors

- Resources to Grow:
  Trust and resilience to face life's challenges; Acceptance to embrace what is here

- Essential Tools:
  All, but especially Flashlight, Door, Beacon

Velcro Problem

- Symptoms:
  Negativity, Unhappiness

- Resources to Grow:
  Gratitude, Joy

- Essential Tools:
  All, but especially Flashlight, Magnifying Glass

Using the Tools to Rewrite Old Programs and Grow Lasting Inner Resources

One of my old, conditioned programs involves being in a state of unease, tension and inner pressure. This manifests itself as an urgency to achieve and get everything done on my to-do list in order to feel all right. This mode of operating in the world and some of the beliefs that grew out of it stemmed in part from my early childhood observations that I got a great deal of attention from adults for achieving. I mistakenly internalized beliefs that I needed to achieve and accomplish things in order to feel seen and loved. This belief came on the heels of my sister's birth when I was four. Feeling vulnerable because she was getting special attention that I wasn't, I discovered that achieving was one way I could guarantee myself some attention. Doing well in school became a way for me to manage this anxiety, but over time it came as a mixed blessing. I was a high achiever and very successful in school, but the need to be recognized in this way became what psychologist Tara Brach refers to as a "false refuge" (Brach, 2013). It brought me recognition, but not true peace within. In fact, there was a lot of insecurity at my core.

This old conditioning became heightened when my mother died. Feeling completely vulnerable and unaware of how to process such a profound loss, I did what I did best; I threw myself into my schoolwork, which was a lot easier to control than my emotions. Besides bringing me recognition and attention through my achievements, it provided me a way to feel safe—by controlling everything that I could in my world. In many ways this served me well, but it also became another false refuge as I created an illusion of control as a way to bypass grappling with my deep grief and my lack of control over my mother's death, and ultimately over my own mortality and those that I love. The gift of working with some wonderful therapists over the years was recognizing and unraveling this old conditioning.

But this old conditioning still sometimes rears its head in my life, and this is where my tools come in handy. First and most fundamentally, the flashlight of mindfulness allows me to recognize when I am pulled into old patterns. A typical way that this old patterning might present itself is in a feeling of frustration or pressure that may come over me when I look at my watch and say to myself "I can't believe it's already 11:00 a.m. and I've hardly gotten anything accomplished today! What's wrong with me?" If unaware, I might continue to push through in a state of tension and unease. But when I use my flashlight, I can see what is happening and recognize that this is an old program. I can feel the tension in my body, notice my constricted breathing, and begin to breathe with more awareness. In this breathing, the tension often eases from my body enough for me to sense some space for a different response.

Taking a few minutes to become mindful, I can recognize the false alarm that is going off, and remind myself there is no real emergency now. This mindful pause can help me return to *this* moment and anchor myself in the present. Recognizing the diet of my own thoughts that are contributing to my stress, I can step back to see a bigger picture (recognizing that much of the pressure I put on myself is self-imposed), and I can become more compassionate with myself. Sometimes if the feelings are intense, it can help to allow them in the door and sit mindfully with them to accept these younger parts of me that still hold anxiety from the past. When those scared or sad parts of me feel seen and heard, they often relax.

Using the magnifying glass, I can then shift my focus to something I feel grateful for in my life. This often brings with it an uplifting feeling and reconnects me with the joy and openness that awaits me in the day. I can also use my beacon as a reminder that acceptance, trust, compassion and gratitude are inner resources available to me as I move through my day.

Julia was a successful businesswoman in her early forties, who struggled with mild anxiety and depression. Despite her outward success, she was filled with self-doubt and inner criticism on a frequent basis. Work became her focus of attention, and she tended to isolate herself socially without realizing it. In addition, while she dated on and off, she often ended relationships before they became too intimate. Julia described that she grew up in a household where her father was hardly around, and her mother worked full time and had four children to raise. While the conditions in which she was raised were not harsh or abusive, she also did not get the warmth and nurturing that she craved. In fact, her mother, who was often depleted by the end of a long day, would frequently come home and express disappointment in the chores her children had left unfinished, instead of asking about Julia's day and offering her positive attention. Her father was working or traveling, and had minimal involvement with her and her siblings.

As Julia began to carry around the flashlight in her day, she recognized that she was often on "high alert," waiting for criticism from her boss, or criticizing herself for not doing enough or doing it well enough. Attending to these alarm signals in her body and the chronic tension that she carried, she recognized that this was an old pattern that had solidified over many decades. Bringing attention to sensations in her body, she recognized a familiar feeling that reminded her of when she was a little girl, wanting to please her mom and feeling uneasy when she couldn't. She also recognized that her mind was often focused on the future, anticipating what *might* happen ("Who might be upset with me? Who might I disappoint today? What will I mess up on?"). When she noticed her mind jumping ahead in this way, she began to practice bringing herself back to the present moment and assessing what was actually happening right then. She was able to recognize that many of the perceived threats were self-created or at least exaggerated, and this allowed her to re-establish some sense of safety and acceptance about *this* moment.

Julia was often her own harshest critic, a voice that she had internalized from childhood and her mother, as well as from herself in an attempt to protect herself from disappointing her mother (If she was hard on herself then maybe she could catch what she was doing "wrong" and fix it before her mother got angry). Recognizing this noisy person in the movie theater of her mind, she began practicing self-compassion for the little girl who just wanted love and approval. Over time, while the critical voice continued to appear, it also softened and Julia was able to develop a healthier diet of thoughts that recognized both her humanness and imperfections, as well as her own competence.

With further work, Julia was able to grieve the loss of the desired mother and father that she never had, and to sit with her anger and sadness about her own unmet needs as a child. She had never directly acknowledged this to herself before. In using the door to embrace her feelings, she recognized that some of the energy she put into holding her feelings at bay also kept her from pursuing intimate relationships for fear of experiencing the disappointment of unmet needs. She began to develop a greater trust in herself for having the capacity to handle her emotions. This freed her to experiment with intimate relationships, knowing that she could handle disappointments that might arise.

Because it was so easy to fall into patterns of self-criticism and fault finding with herself, Julia found the magnifying glass helped her to notice and highlight her own strengths and competence, and to accept positive feedback and warmth from others that she might otherwise have dismissed. What she most wanted was connection, and her beacon became a daily reminder for her to make choices that aligned with this. She began reaching out to others, making a point to sit with coworkers at lunch, and making plans on the weekend to engage in social activities.

An Exercise to Help You Unhook from Old Programs

When you feel uncomfortable emotions in a given situation, see if you can step away and take a mindful pause (using your flashlight). Bring your attention into your body and feel the sensations that are present. Name your emotions and see if you might be with them in a compassionate way (using the door). Ask yourself if any of these emotions feel like they are connected to an earlier time in your life or remind you of how you felt as a child or adolescent. If so, see if you might imagine sitting with that younger child or adolescent the way that a loving parent would sit with their child, in an attentive, present and compassionate way.

Now draw or imagine two boxes of varying sizes. The first box represents how much of your emotions are connected to the present situation at hand. The second box represents how much of your current emotional experience is connected to an earlier time in your life, or an event or situation that occurred when you were younger. For example, if a couple is fighting and one partner pauses to be mindful and imagine these boxes, he/she might recognize that much of their anger is being triggered by being reminded of a critical parent growing up. So three-quarters of their anger may belong in this large box of early childhood experiences, while only one-quarter of the anger belongs in the much smaller box corresponding to actual upset at their partner for hurting their feelings.

As another example, a person at a party may realize no one is talking to them and interpret the situation as evidence that they are disliked or looked down upon. When examining their boxes, however, they might realize that most of these emotions of rejection stem from early experiences of being bullied as a child, while only a small proportion of their emotions are related to the current social situation.

Once you recognize the size of each of your boxes, see if you can use your flashlight to focus your attention back on the "present moment box." From this place of presence, you are free to choose how best to respond. Use your beacon to guide you toward wise and helpful actions.

More Thoughts About Unhooking from Old, Automatic Programs

While it may help to understand where our habitual emotional and behavioral patterns come from (for example, early childhood or other experiences), this is not always essential to unhook from these automatic programs. What is most important is *awareness* that we are operating from an automatic program in the first place, an ability to drop into our bodies and into the present moment, and an opportunity to establish a felt sense of something new as we choose a more intentional response. Self-compassion can be especially helpful to allow us to embrace whatever we are experiencing, recognize our common humanity, and observe our emotions, thoughts and impulses from a place of kindness rather than from a place of self-criticism or judgment ("What's wrong with me that I'm feeling this way!"). When we can observe our automatic behaviors with mindful awareness and compassion for our difficulties, we gain greater flexibility to choose a response that will best serve us, and free ourselves from our habitual conditioning.

The awareness, acceptance, and leaning toward the pleasant and unpleasant alike that is discussed in this book takes courage, skill, patience, repetition and practice. As we touch into and embrace our authenticity and the fullness of our life as it is right now, we also make space to hold our suffering, vulnerabilities and shortcomings. To live a full life and experience wholeness, I believe we must acknowledge and accept both sides of this coin. The alternative to this is stagnation, complacency, automaticity, and limitation. The freedom that results from embracing both sides of the coin and using our tools to unhook from old conditioned programs of childhood *and* automatic evolutionary responses is well worth the effort. Unlike a quick fix that has an end point, this is an ongoing commitment to ourselves, each day, to be awake, alive, and living in line with our values.

This last exercise that follows can be used often to help you work through the day-to-day challenges that arise. It combines and integrates all of the five tools discussed in this book. At first, it will help to pick small situations in which to try this, but with practice, you can begin to use this exercise even during more difficult situations as they are unfolding. Each time you do this, you grow the inner resources of safety, presence, self-compassion, perspective, trust, acceptance, gratitude and joy—all of which you can then draw on to help you with future challenges that will arise.

An Exercise to Practice Growing Inner Resources to Unhook from Old Patterns

Think about a habitual response pattern or behavior that shows up for you in a typical week that is not so helpful (for example, being self-critical, engaging in an unhelpful behavior such as overeating, yelling when you are upset, or something else).

Think of a typical situation in which you might be triggered and pulled into this automatic response pattern. Imagine that situation is happening now (be sure to pick something that is not too upsetting or intense; choose a day-to-day stressor that is not too overwhelming).

1. As you imagine that situation happening, take a moment to notice that you are being triggered. Shine your flashlight on what is unfolding. See yourself stepping out of a mind-wandering mode, into the present moment. Notice if you are perceiving a threat, if your false alarm is going off. Bring your awareness to your breathing and recognize that you are safe in this moment. Take some time to feel this safety in your body.

2. Now notice any unhealthy thoughts that you might be feeding yourself. Notice whether your thoughts are contributing to the difficulty of the situation in any way (whether you might be criticizing yourself, or looking inaccurately at the situation in some way). Observe the situation from the farthest possible vantage point. Send yourself compassion for whatever you are experiencing. Acknowledge that the situation is difficult.

3. Allow yourself to be with whatever emotions arise. Welcome them in the door. It is OK to feel however you feel. Imagine how you would sit with a good friend going through something similar, with acceptance and non-judgment.

4. When it feels right for you, and only after you have spent enough time for yourself on step three, use your magnifying glass to find some positivity that you might have overlooked. It might be a positive aspect about the situation that is occurring; it might be a strength in yourself that you can focus on; it might be the heartfelt support of others; or it might involve summoning a feeling that would be helpful in this moment, such as calmness, patience or equanimity. Whatever you choose to magnify, feel this positivity in your body. You do not need to get rid of any difficult feelings; just invite in the positivity.

5. Think about your beacon. What is most important to you, what do you most value in yourself, and how do you want to behave that aligns with those values? Allow this to guide you to respond to the situation at hand in a skillful manner.

Concluding Thoughts

When I think about what it means for me to re-awaken and come home to who I am, I immediately recall a scene from my house in Michigan when I was about three or four years old. My father would often play folk or classical music and I would dance joyfully around the living room. I remember not just the image of this, but the feeling of being that little girl, being "moved" by the music, and sensing a playful surrender and carefreeness of spirit where I could fully express myself without worrying about impressing others or being good enough or achieving something. I felt a freedom and aliveness in those moments, and when I experience that now in my adult life, it feels like being home.

↩

~ Is there a time in your childhood when you recall being content, at peace, joyful, or complete in some way?

~ When do you experience that in your adult life, and what helps you do so?

When we learn to unhook from our thoughts and feelings (and recognize they are part of our internal mental experience but not the whole of who we are), and when we can observe and understand the primitive tendencies of our reacting brain, without being driven by these, this allows us to sense into a wholeness that is available to all of us. Dr. Daniel Siegel has studied how setting aside regular time to reflect inwardly (with practices such as mindful awareness, and what he calls "Mindsight"), can actually enable us to grow brain fibers that link differentiated parts of our brain to create a more integrated brain. When we experience brain integration, there is an experience of harmony, as opposed to chaos and rigidity that might otherwise exist (Siegel, 2015).

Imagine for a moment that all of the parts of you—your scared self, the part of you that feels unworthy, the thoughts that say "I can't do this," as well as the parts of you that feel competent, courageous, confident, strong and joyful—are all instruments in an orchestra. Now imagine that there was no conductor, and that some of the more "difficult" parts, such as your scared self or thoughts of unworthiness, were playing so loudly that they thought that they were all alone on stage. That might sound pretty disconnected and disharmonious. You might sense that something feels missing or incomplete. When we are hooked into old automatic programs, and driven by more primitive, reactive networks of our brain, it can feel like this.

Now envision that you are not any one instrument, but the conductor, and you step on stage and begin to mindfully direct the instruments. You are able to recognize that each instrument is separate, and yet each is connected to a larger whole. You are not identified with any one particular instrument, but see all of them as interconnected. You would not think of getting rid of any instruments, but instead you honor all of them as members of the orchestra. When the instruments start playing together, there is a synchrony and harmony that becomes a beautiful piece of music. You as the conductor can step back and watch all of this unfold as you gently guide what is already there to evolve into its full potential. Eventually, you are able to step back further and recognize that you are not even the conductor, but are one with the music itself—your own unique piece of music that has always been there, waiting to be revealed.

It is my intention that the tools in this book will offer you a window into this experience of becoming the conductor, and ultimately the music itself; and will help you to discover who you already are.

Remember, life is always a work in progress, and there is no end point of perfection to strive for. Life will continue to throw you challenges, but you have tools that you can bring with you to face those challenges with greater resilience. There is only arriving in this moment, and embracing the whole of yourself—your strengths and your imperfections, the messiness and the beauty of this life—as you dance on the tight rope and come home to your own open heart.

References

Brach, T. (2013). *True refuge: Finding peace and freedom in your own awakened heart.* New York: Bantom Books.

Brooks, R.B. & Goldstein, S. (2001*). Raising resilient children: Fostering strength, hope and optimism in your child.* Lincolnwood, IL: Contemporary Books.

Brown, B. (2017, June 22). Shame shields: The armor we use to protect ourselves and why it doesn't serve us. Pesi Seminars [online program]. Retrieved from: https://www.pesi.com/blog/details/1234/brené-brown-on-the-danger-of-unspoken-shame

Edwards, K. (2017). What Are You Rehearsing?. *Psych Central.* Retrieved on June 27, 2018, from https://psychcentral.com/blog/what-are-you-rehearsing/

Goleman, D. (1995). *Emotional intelligence: Why it can matter more than IQ.* New York, NY: Bantam Books.

Gollwitzer, P.M., & Sheeran, P. (2006). Implementation intentions and goal achievement: A meta-analysis of effects and processes. *Advances in Experimental and Social Psychology, 38* (69-119).

Halliwell, E. (2017). The science and practice of staying present through difficult times. *Mindful.* Retrieved from https://www.mindful.org/science-practice-staying-present-difficult-times/

Hanson, R. (2014-2015). The foundations of well-being: Growing the good in your brain and your life [online program]. Retrieved from https://www.thefoundationsofwellbeing.com.

Hanson, R. (2013*). Hardwiring happiness: The new brain science of con tentment, calm and confidence.* New York, NY: Harmony Books.

Hanson, R. (2016). Positive Neuroplasticity Training [online program]. Retrieved from: http://www.rickhanson.net/positive-neuroplasticity-training/

Hanson, R. (2016). Professional Course in Positive Neuroplasticity [on line program]. Retrieved from: http://www.rickhanson.net/professional-course-positive-neuroplasticity/

Hanson, R. & Hanson, F. (2018). *Resilient: How to grow an unshakeable core of calm, strength, and happiness.* New York: Harmony Books.

Hanson, R., & Mendius, R.(2009). *Buddha's brain: The practical neuroscience of happiness, love & wisdom.* Oakland, CA: New Harbinger Publications.

Hayes, S.C. & Smith, S. (2005). *Get out of your mind & into your life: The new acceptance and commitment therapy.* Oakland, CA: New Harbinger Publications.

Kabat-Zinn, J. (1994). *Wherever you go there you are: Mindfulness meditation in everyday life.* New York, NY: Hyperion.

Kenison, K. (2009). *The gift of an ordinary day.* New York: Grand Central Publishing.

Killingsworth, M., & Gilbert, D. (2010). A wandering mind is an unhappy mind. *Science*, 330 (6006), 932.

MacKinnon, M. (2017). *Neuroscience of mindfulness: Default mode network, meditation, & mindfulness.* Retrieved from: https://www.mindfulnessmd.com/2014/07/08/neuroscience-of-mindfulness-default-mode-network-meditation-mindfulness/

McGonigal, K. *The neuroscience of change: A compassion-based program for personal transformation.* Sounds True, 2017. Audiobook.

McGonigal, K. (2017, March 21). The neuroscience of change. Sounds True Neuroscience Training Summit. Retrieved from: https://www.soundstrue.com/store/neuroscience-training-summit-2017?sq=1#jumplink-presenters

Neff, K. D. & Germer, C. (2017). Self-Compassion and psychological wellbeing. In J. Doty (Ed.) *Oxford Handbook of Compassion Science,* Chap. 27. Oxford University Press.

Newberg, A., and Waldman, M. (2013). *Words can change your brain: 12 conversation strategies to build trust, resolve conflict, and increase intimacy.* New York, NY: Penguin.

Segal, Z. (2016). Mindfulness changes how we process sadness.*Mindful.* Retrieved from https://www.mindful.org/mindfulness-changes-how-we-process-sadness/

Siegel, D.J. (2010). The science of mindfulness. *Mindful.* Retrieved from: https://www.mindful.org/the-science-of-mindfulness/

Siegel, D. J. (2014). *Brainstorm: The power and purpose of the teenage brain.* New York, NY: Penguin.

Siegel, D.J. (2015). *Mindsight: The new science of personal transformation.* New York, NY: Bantam Books.

Siegel, D. J. (2017). Why mind-wandering can be a detriment to happiness. Retrieved from https://www.nicabm.com/why-mind-wandering-can-be-a-detriment-to-happiness-and-one-way-to-refocus-2/

Siegel, D.J. (2017). Using daily mindfulness to enhance your brain: An interview with Daniel Siegel. [Interview]. Retrieved from https://1440.org/using-daily-mindfulness-enhance-brain-interview-daniel-siegel/

Siegel, R.D. *(2010). The mindfulness solution: Everyday practices for everyday problems.* New York, NY: The Guilford Press.

Waldman, M. (2014). 10 mind blowing discoveries about the human brain. Retrieved from: http://launchmoxie.com/wp-content/uploads/downloads//1-NeuroWisdom-Ebook.pdf

Index

A

acceptance, 38, 83, 130, 134, 138, 139
  self- 97,
Acceptance and Commitment Therapy (ACT), 23–25, 26, 110
acronyms
  stress, 56
  unhook, 77
  door, 91
anger, 40, 50, 81–84, 86, 87–90, 92, 103, 125, 136, 137,
  acceptance of, 6
  embracing, 57
  in Acceptance and Commitment Therapy, 26
  parenting, 125, 137
anxiety, *xiii*, 6, 12, 16, 23, 81, 115, 131, 134
attention *(see also mindfulness)*
  in *"stuck dial"*, 17
  quality of 38, 40–50, 62, 65, 70, 72, 75, 95, 122
authentic happiness, 20, 132
automatic pilot, 19, 38
autonomic nervous system, 52

B

balance, 2–3, 7, 36, 52, 69
  in healthy thoughts, 76
  Pie Chart exercise, 76
Brach, Tara, ix, 66, 72, 82, 133, 143
brain
  amygdala, 63
  brain science, 75, 112
  changes, 43, 95
  evolution of, 12, 28–30
  in mind-wandering, 18, 22
  plasticity, 34
  reactive, 12–15, 140, 141
breathing, mindful, 43, 51
  practice exercise, 56, 138–139

ABOUT THE AUTHOR

 **Beth Kurland, PhD.,** is a licensed clinical psychologist, author and public speaker, with over 20 years of experience working with people across the lifespan from preschoolers through adults. With a strong interest and expertise in using mind-body practices, she is passionate about teaching people practical tools to create greater well-being and wholeness in their lives.

Beth is the author of the award-winning books: *The Transformative Power of Ten Minutes: An Eight Week Guide to Reducing Stress and Cultivating Well-Being,* a Finalist of the Next Generation Indie Book Awards in the Health and Wellness category, and *Gifts of the Rain Puddle: Poems, Meditations and Reflections for the Mindful Soul,* Winner of the Next Generation Indie Book Awards in the Gift/Novelty category.

Inspired by the journeys of hundreds of her patients, as well as lessons from her own life and teachings from psychology and neuroscience, Beth invites readers to discover what is possible when they transcend the habits of their mind and awaken to their fullest life.

For free audio and video meditations, and other resources, please visit Beth's website:
BethKurland.com

WELLBRIDGE BOOKS™
an imprint of Six Degrees Publishing Group

"Bridges to Health & Wellness for the Whole Person through Creative, Solution-Oriented Books"